THE WELL-PAID CHRISTIAN

A SPIRIT-CENTERED GUIDE TO SHOWING UP AS
YOUR BEST SELF IN SOCIETY

LAUREN AHMADIAN

CONTENTS

1. The Dilemma and the Dream   1
2. A Professional?   11
3. The Framework   25
4. The Business of Ministry   29
5. Remember Who You Are   45
6. Follow Your Intuition   53
7. Integrating the Studies   73
8. Understanding Society   93
9. The Closeup – Wholeness,   117
   Communication, Business
10. Who to Follow – Finding Inspiration   127
11. Nothing Is Lacking – Peace   135
12. Building Together with Our King and   141
    Priest

About the Author   147
About Difference Press   149
Other Books by Difference Press   153
Thank You   155

To God the Father. He has educated, provided for, and protected me. To God the Son, to Whom I am engaged to be married by the Holy Spirit: here is to our wedding day, the marriage of Christ and His Church, when the fullness of Time is here.

THE DILEMMA AND THE DREAM

"Stand by the ways and see and ask for the ancient paths where the good way is and walk in it and you will find rest for your souls."

— JEREMIAH 6:16, NASB

ISABEL'S JOURNEY

"Today as you listen, this Scripture has been fulfilled" (Luke 4:21, NASB). With this proclamation, that He was in fact the Messiah, Jesus, the Son of God, began his ministry being known as the son of Joseph, the Jewish carpenter. He had spent his entire adult life up until that point learning both of his "fathers'" trades. From age twelve to thirty, as was the Jewish tradition of that time, he learned carpentry, his father Joseph's trade, and he developed ministry, his father God's "trade" as a human.

Oftentimes in our Christian ministries here on earth, the subject of Biblical Scriptures and their importance is reiterated, discussed, etc. What are the Scriptures God has deposited into you? Which ones are the stamps upon your skin, the imprints on your soul, and the notes of your spirit? Have you answered the call of these Scriptures? Did the answered interpretations come out differently than you first estimated?

Isabel is a civil engineer. Well, at least that is what she studied at university. She also believes ministry is the ultimate way to serve Jesus.

Her parents heard the call of God to move from the larger city to an offbeat one and asked Isabel to join them. At the time, it seemed like the most relevant option. What else was she to do? Her indecision at her life's career direction "forced" her to make a rapid choice for her livelihood. So she joined the ministry with her parents at the local church in the new city, and life has not been the same for her since. While her heart seems more and more fulfilled by the progress made in other people's lives because of her work, her spirit seems more and more filled with unease that something is not right, and her mind seems to be never still. She has the desire to build things – tangible buildings.

Humorously, Isabel's "hearing from God" never seemed to be listened to or accepted by her parents.

People in school and at the university loved it, for the most part. Some called her crazy, but she learned to identify them before sharing any "helpful" information and to weigh her options before speaking. She's always been aware of her prophetic gifts. However, this gift has always made her feel as if she was unable to fit in in whichever arena she found herself. There's always been a conflict between her heart and mind – two contenders fighting for her attention and commitment, seemingly unreconcilable.

She either wants to passionately serve Jesus with ministry, or she wants to turn all her dreams into real, tangible results as a businesswoman. She feels conflicted in every way. But the real and most pressing problem on her mind is: how is she going to pay her bills? She feels that if she could just focus on one direction, then finances would not be an issue.

Should she jump out on her own as a prophetic minister (only her father thinks such things are still possible), or should she start a full-time career doing something with real-estate or similar (her mother is more inclined toward this)?

THE DILEMMA

Does Isabel's story resonate with you? Is life fragmented for you, also? Do you wish everything could just fall into place? You love the business world. What happened to that desire? You would like whichever career you choose to help you show up as your best self in society. Is this what you believe ministry to be?

Your biggest wish is to see heaven on earth. You have heard many ministers paint pictures of what this means, how it can be accomplished, and where we must take our place in order to do so. There always seemed to be some small – or at times large – pieces missing from these dissertations or conversations on stage. You turn to the Lord and ask Him His perspective. He only seems to give you more visions of buildings, cities, countries, leaders, constructions, or other seemingly "off-the-point" topics. You may have even asked a few trusted friends, but they seem to only paint pictures of a reality that can be sustained through doing church ministry.

Sleeping at night is not always easy. Waking in the morning is only easy if it is a workday. Your inner conflict is starting to take its toll on your health and ability to lead a full life.

You have read in the Scriptures that a "double-minded man should not think that he will receive anything from the Lord" (James 1:5-8, NASB), so you wonder how it is you are to become single-minded. And why does it seem you have two completely "opposing" dreams within you? You know that you can only ask God for "the fruit of your hands" (Psalm 128:2, ESV, Proverbs 12:14, NASB, Proverbs 31:16, ESV, Proverbs 31:31, NKJV) if indeed your hands are put to a work that you are meant to be doing.

You feel the strong need for alignment, but no one and no group has truly felt like home. You want the chiropractic adjustment to all your fears, longings, dreams, gifts, history, and culture. No book or conference or acquaintance has quite convinced you of which choice to take, and conversations with yourself and the Holy Spirit only seem to leave your head spinning.

Now, here you are, late twenties or early thirties, feeling stuck in the same dilemma you had in your late teens: what do I do with my life?

If you could just *pick* one direction, go all in, never look back, and wake up satisfied each morning, then perhaps you would no longer be concerned about the fact that you seemingly have wasted so much energy and time.

Satisfaction. Delight. Peace. Wouldn't it be nice to feel as though your heart and thoughts were always in alignment with each other? Do you really want to wait another day and wake up one morning to see that more time and energy and never-met friends still elude you?

What is your best self in society? You would like to be that woman. You seem to have two continuing images of yourself that lead two very different lives. You have even considered spending half your life committed to one career (either ministry or business), retiring, and then committing the second half of your life the other career. But it sounds exhausting for what seems like your already exhausted life.

THE DREAM

Wouldn't it be lovely to live in a gorgeous house with God in heaven and just administrate with Him everything you want to see happen on earth? Buildings here. Infrastructure here. Parks here. People listening to the "correct" prophecy here. Kindness and wealth there.

Wealth. You can't make up your mind which side of the Christian "argument" you agree with here.

You often consider the statement Jesus made while on earth: "I came not to abolish the law, but to fulfill it" (Matthew 5:17). It has always intrigued you.

You want to be a better leader as a woman with very different aspects of her life than most around her.

You want to measure your results as a woman who influences.

You want to understand how to be a woman who loves Jesus and a woman who sees herself as an influencer in some capacity to some very specific audience yet to be met.

You don't want to feel pointless everywhere you go, especially when you have this deep sense that everywhere you go, you are somehow supposed to be deeply impacting everyone and everything. What is that sense?

You want to be accepted as a cultured and intelligent woman who follows Jesus without feeling judged, condemned, or worse, rebuked. Rebuked for wrong things is fine. But rebuked for what is constantly in your head, in your heart, and deep within your belly? Surely God would not give you such prophetic gifts and such grand building business dreams if you were not meant to use them?

And the most urgent result you desire to see once you make your decision and commit yourself is finances starting to fall in. You would think that after five years in the ministry, something would have started already in the financial realm. You want to use the talents and dreams that you have been given, but you want to have a life of no regrets, one that was truly given as a beautiful, fragrant offering.

Everywhere you turn, there seems to be some different explanation about reality itself, God's callings, and what it actually means to live the life of both yours and God's dreams.

It would be wonderful to know: what does He want from you?

It would be so wonderful to know: what is the best use of everything you have been given?

Maybe the only one who cares so much about these things is yourself, but God would not be so distant would He?

OUR INTRODUCTION

I realize I have not introduced myself.

Today is the day we are going to begin a process together, if you will allow me to take you on what may seem at times an unrelated journey. Together, we are going to walk through a new skillset. A new realm of possibilities.

Will you allow me to show you some possibilities? You already feel as if you have heard and seen everything except what you really want to hear and see, so maybe we can try something new together.

What if we kept only your gifts and desires in mind for now and made everything else as a white whiteboard? What if we put all of your questions, all other people's ideas, all of your current perceptions, all teachings from others – whether encouraging or discouraging – and all other floating decisions onto a whiteboard? Write it down in marker, and then erase everything.

Picture it with me for a moment. Whether you need to slowly erase all of the words or just look for a while at a white, freshly erased, whiteboard. No words. No input. Yet. I encourage you to not consider anything else *except you and God* for an extended space.

You are loved. After going through this book, I have confidence that you will have a growing strong conviction of how to show up as your best self in society. And whether you finally agree with what I have presented to you or not is actually not my goal. My goal is to affect you in such a way that you will know what *you* believe, take what *God* has told you, and go in a strong, firm, decision-making direction for the rest of your life *based on who God created you to be.*

This book will present to you a skillset. After going through this skillset, you will probably find yourself with many new and refreshing outlets in society.

I am going to remind you to trust some things which you already have.

We will surely take you to your desired destination if you are willing to trust what I share. In the next chapter, I will share a part of my own journey and how I arrived at the desired destination. I am here to tell you it can be done.

CHAPTER SUMMARY

- You want to be seen and known for who you uniquely are, and you would like the fulfillment of living your purpose in your daily life.
- You feel your career choice indecision has negatively affected the flow of finances into your life.

Where to Start

- With a freshly erased "whiteboard," as mentioned in the exercise, be still and quiet. Enjoy the freedom of having everything that has caused you confusion erased.

2

A PROFESSIONAL?

*"I am the vine, you are the branches; he who abides in Me
and I in him, he bears much fruit, for apart from Me you
can do nothing."*

— JOHN 15:5, NASB

How can I help you? I could not reach a satisfying result for this exact dilemma for probably well over a decade. I do not wish the same for you. Nor do I wish two lifetimes and two retirements for you. But if either the former situation or latter is true for you, do not fear! The best is yet to come.

First, a little about my previous experiences and background: I had a great education, I have always educated myself for fun in my spare time, and I have always spent my time and gained friendships from people of many different cultures and backgrounds and places in life. As a single person throughout college, I spent weeks, months, years, on four different continents, immersed in two different language groups different than my native, and with persons of varying economic and cultural backgrounds. My life has been filled with adventures, highly-extenuating circumstances, and a continuous string of others' perspectives to broaden my horizons. "The best is yet to come" truly when we are at a tipping point in our identity, and everything poured into us begins to pour out in one continuous stream of refreshing water.

I have been there. Issues repeating in my head, hours over magazines and books. I knew what I wanted to see. I knew what I wanted to do. These two just didn't seem to agree.

Which is why my head was always spinning.

For myself, having come from a gift and talent overload background, my struggle was the same as yours: what do I do with all of these? Are they even coordinated? And how do I make sure I properly manage everything I've been given and not lose it?

I had been well-immersed in prophetic training straight from the Father, Son, and Holy Spirit, and I had sought out encouragement from similar persons.

I had been well-educated in school, educated myself for fun outside of school with a "forever-learning" motto, and always had a friend from a different culture.

With every side-job I had during college and after college, I viewed the entire business as my ministry.

With every friend or peer-group or family member, I was constantly discerning, prophesying, preaching, listening, sharing, empathizing.

And the professors of any artistic class I took which happened to discuss society or understanding people within society seemed to relate to some of my dreams and took a great interest in me also. They said I had real talent and would sit in awe. One even said he wished he could pay me to continue with such talent.

But they all seemed to notice one thing: my attentions were split. I was holding myself back.

Throughout my life, I have always felt this pull.

Growing up, I was continually immersed in sights, sounds, words, visions, smells, feelings, unctions, etc. *God talked to me all the time.* All the time.

It wasn't until my twenties that I figured out that most people in the Christian church either do not accept these gifts, do not have these gifts, or continually close the door on their own similar gifts.

People outside the Christian church almost always have two responses to these sort of gifts (if you let on that you have them). One, they are freaked out and think you are crazy. Two, they are so helped and excited by them that their life radically changes for the better.

So I had to learn, seeking out "mentors" through online programs, online teachings, and various books that seemed to take decades to find.

Really, the only thing that seemed to help for the first thirty years of my life was everything found in the Bible. It was all there. I just had to have real conversations with God and try to keep records of as much as I could.

DREAMS

As a child, I played businesswoman occasionally, pored over interior design and fashion books, studied "experts," and dreamt of building great buildings and having all of the money in the world to build whatever I wanted without having to hold back because of my finances.

There were the strange mixes of my dreams about buildings and businesses and my visions from God regarding spiritual movements, etc. I started to notice I knew things automatically. Not because it was one of the hundreds of topics I had taught myself on growing up or because someone else had said something and I remembered it. No, I just seemed to start knowing things. Things about the details of my dreams.

I could walk past a building and suddenly would see images of a team who put it together, and I would begin to consider if the way it was built was the best use of the budget provided to that main developer. I would see the material used, the way the building was built in that district, would realize how old or young the construction was, and how it was maintaining its sturdiness and quality. If I were to mention such thoughts to persons who actually worked with investors, architects, and developers, I would be listened to and what I had to say would be considered.

How did I know if these facts were indeed true?

First, since it started to happen so frequently, and I had already tested every other prophetic gift I had been given, I believed it was probably true. God never lies (as a belief), and God had never lied to me (as an experience! and it had been an experience).

But really, it was when I started being mistaken by random people as someone who had years-worth of expertise in certain areas that were not related to my degree. I remember when one gentleman, who looked to be a construction worker, turned around at a line in a bank and said to me something similar to, "You are an expert on framing, aren't you?" And he tried to start getting me a job with the company he was working for.

You have similar experiences. Whether it is with real-estate, architecture, construction, or other areas of business, there are certain facts, outside of what you learned in your degree, that you seem to keep getting pictures of in your mind or messages from God about.

You are not alone.

THE DECISION

I remember one day at the library after work, several years before I met my husband and started working with him, I saw a beautiful modern architecture building, complete with the many large windows. It burned something so deep within me; it seemed to surpass even my desire to be married and have children. It seemed so necessary.

Most people outside of the Christian church would, if they were bold enough and without other commitments, probably take such recurring dreams and actually go start a career in some aspect of such deep longings.

But then there are people such as you and I, who have felt at one point that we did not have permission. And so many in Western Christian ministry talk about the highest call to steward what you have been given for the benefit of others to hear the gospel and follow. The widespread belief has been why else would the Lord give you such gifts unless you were meant to be like one of the great modern prophets – writing, speaking, holding conferences, and building a ministry completely surrounding all of this input you are receiving from God? Isn't that what those of us in the ministry do? Receive from the Lord, and pour out to others?

Why is it, then, that two such seemingly different life callings would be placed within one person?

For a while, particularly all throughout my twenties, I struggled with this question. Feeling like I was wasting time, holding myself back, letting God down, letting the world down, and never knowing which direction to finally plunge forward in. So I kept small jobs to pay the bills, spent my energy and priorities on ministry, and then with any leftover time, I would browse architecture websites, study interior design magazines (only the very top-notch from the highest in Europe or similar usually), etc.

I had been doing ministry as a single woman from the time I was nineteen until the time I was twenty-nine, but before that I was still at least 50 percent of the time in ministry "mode" with my family and peer group: ministering to them, preaching, listening, and basically spending all of my energy in trying to see those around me made whole.

When I finally started actually working with a real-estate investor, who had actually studied these things and had actually been involved in several work projects or business partners of similar areas (real-estate development, construction management, architecture, and similar), it turns out everything I just "knew" was exactly spot-on. So spot-on that seemingly only top experts in the industry seemed to be aware of the knowledge which seemed to just grow out of my blood.

Now, I currently have already spent two and half years working with a real-estate investor. I have been able to do market research and meet up with vendors for our investment in a foreign country, and I even was able to manage a flip and simple design of a condo in a foreign country.

Interestingly enough, after I had picked the very spot in which we had purchased our investment properties, it was named the number one place to retire in 2020. The 2017 foreign investment off the Silver Coast of Portugal also turned out to be the easiest, most lovely, and most cost-efficient and safe bet for a foreign real-estate investment of small size.

The point is, I have had exposure, experience, and opportunities which ten years ago I only thought about.

But thinking about taking the business cards offered to you and starting a new career and actually stepping out to change one's entire life are two different things.

What made me take the jump? Why didn't I stay in ministry?

And if I finally decided to take the jump, why didn't I take it sooner? Why, one year when I was about twenty-two in the library after work/college classes, staring at the marvelous architecture, did I not take the jump then? And wasn't it all maybe a metaphor? Maybe all of those real-estate facts I just knew were "types and pictures" same as everything in the Old Testament is a "type and a picture." Maybe I was just supposed to be a prophetic minister building lots of ministry "real-estate," a glorious project for Jesus? Yes? Some persons tried to convince me that my dreams were metaphors only and that I should go into full-time ministry, developing lots of "real-estate" in the spiritual realm.

But this answer didn't entirely satisfy me. And it doesn't satisfy you either. And no amazing minister, amazing prophet, or amazing real-estate developer seems to have given you the exact answer you are looking for yet, have they?

If you are willing to take the journey with me, I can take you through a process that took me decades to understand.

And perhaps, along the way, you will suddenly not only have your a-ha moment, but you will also have some invaluable insight which I can learn from you.

Because you not only have gifts and dreams, you are a brilliant person. You love to discover new things. You love to see the best come out of people. You love to see the best come out in the world around you. And this is why I made the decision I did. Not only with the Lord and for my own growing, but for people like you.

We were put onto earth as humans for a reason. The first job assignment, God's job to Adam to name all the creatures, was a very "lively" job. It was all about life. God did not tell Adam to go tell every creature that God exists. All of creation already knows this. God told Adam to participate in the discovery of the earth around him – God told Adam to creatively name every creature that lived around him! And then Adam started to wonder what was wrong with him and why he didn't have a mate like so many of the creatures did, so God created Eve. God didn't tell Adam, "What you have asked for is an unholy thing." No, God even said that it is not good for a man to be alone. The whole of Scripture must be taken into context as a whole concept. We cannot pull out bits and pieces and interpret the purpose without understanding the *whole.*

This is why I ended up making the decision I did. God wanted me to *live.* God wanted me to be *whole.* He did not want me to be a "doctor" for broken persons. He wanted me to be an example of a whole person. Because if the only example people have is "doctors" (ministers), they would assume that being a doctor is what it means to be healthy. No, being healthy is what it means to be healthy. A doctor is there for extenuating circumstances. And actually ministry, or *the administration of God's grace,* is similar to the administration of resources in a government: it is there to put some resources here, some resources there. It is there to allocate some investments here and some investments there.

So the best ministry is to appropriately administer the resources God has invested into your life. Did He give you gifts? Did He give you dreams? Well, let's administer these graces, or gifts, appropriately and purely and waste nothing as we discover the reality around us!

The process that I have gone through over a long period of time, I have condensed and am sharing now with you. The answers that I have been given all in a moment, I am expanding upon and explaining here with you. Whether long process or short, I will try to share all on a similar plain here for you, and I believe it will be a help to you or, at the very least, encourage you towards your own convictions. At the very most, I believe that what I share will help you to make a decision and feel good about it, trusting all the fullness that will follow it.

So let's start this journey of self-discovery and alignment.

CHAPTER SUMMARY

- I spent almost a decade in ministry among many different kinds of people. I transitioned into business, and have spent roughly two-three years in an industry I care about.
- Take note, I did not mention finances once.

Where to Start

- Meditate, or think deeply and slowly, in a quiet and undisturbed place, concerning John 15:1-11 ("I am the true vine, and my

Father is the gardener. [2] He cuts off every branch in me that bears no fruit, while every branch that does bear fruit, he prunes so that it will be even more fruitful. [3] You are already clean because of the word I have spoken to you. [4] Remain in me as I also remain in you. No branch can bear fruit by itself; it must remain in the vine. Neither can you bear fruit unless you remain in me.

- [5] "I am the vine; you are the branches. If you remain in me and I in you, you will bear much fruit; apart from me you can do nothing. [6] If you do not remain in me, you are like a branch that is thrown away and withers; such branches are picked up, thrown into the fire, and burned. [7] If you remain in me and my words remain in you, ask whatever you wish, and it will be done for you. [8] This is to my Father's glory, that you bear much fruit, showing yourselves to be my disciples.

- [9] "As the Father has loved me, so have I loved you. Now remain in my love. [10] If you keep my commands, you will remain in my love, just as I have kept my Father's commands and remain in his love. [11] I have told you this so that my joy may be in you and that your joy may be complete." [NASB]). You may consider several different versions or translations, yes, but more importantly, which phrases resonate within you? Which phrases resound or reverberate within you?

3

THE FRAMEWORK

In this book, we are going to grow, test, remember, change, and implement as I present some ideas that you can acquire into new perceptions. You can choose to acquire new perspectives as you read through each chapter.

We will be building concepts one on the other, so it is recommended that you read the chapters in the order they are presented so that you can come to the best results for yourself. The presented ideas in each chapter will be opening up concepts for better decision-making, not only for day-to-day choices, but ultimately, for the life-changing choices such as which career to follow.

At the start of each chapter, we will most often have a scripture from the Bible as well as a talk regarding yourself, your current situation, and the wishes you are searching for.

Then, we will present a topic; perhaps one you are already familiar with, or perhaps one that you have never considered. The topic will most likely end with some sort of practical implementation for yourself in your daily life, some questions you may have about the topic, and a summary.

Are you ready? And just so you know, this process can be adjusted as time goes on if you apply it later in life as well, so long as the key takeaways are remembered.

We will be going through a process together so that you can feel confident in your career choice by the end. We will be going through almost a pendulum swing of sorts: chapters 4 and 5 will be an up-swing of altitude, as we will actually shift your question of "what should my career be?" to something else entirely (so that we can more satisfactorily arrive at the solution you are looking for).

Chapter 6 is the key pivot point from the first half of our process together in deciding on your career, and together, both chapters 6 and 7 will be the "heavy lifting" of the process, where we will actually work on an entire perspective shift.

Chapters 8 and 9 will be the start of a new beginning with this newly acquired perspective. Chapters 8 and 9 will be about society. Chapters 10 and 11 will be about you becoming your best self in society; they will be about how you can apply your newly acquired perspective. Chapter 12 will be our goodbye, for now.

Each chapter will be presented so that the material may be taken in bite-size pieces for easier digestion. It will also hopefully make it easier to go back and find a previous topic.

So, as we begin this process, let's start a little slowly. The following four chapters will be regarding certain ideas of which you are already aware. However, maybe these ideas have not been discussed in the way which we will consider them here in this book.

MY LETTER TO YOU: THE CONSTELLATION

Dear Friend,

You have a place. Yours is a unique place. Yours is a valuable place.

I trust you because God trusts you. He has entrusted you with much, and I believe you will bring forth good fruit.

You can fit anywhere you like in the world because you already have this skill set to do so. Even if you do not feel especially close to any one group, you will find your place. That is part of the journey we are going on together! The rest of this journey will actually be in discovering fresh, new perspectives for fresh new places.

Friend, your place and everyone's place in society do in fact affect each other, but not often in the way we think.

You will find that perhaps society is exactly like what you believed deeply within you – completely different from what those around you teach, preach, or adamantly climb to the tops of mountains to discover.

We will talk about peace versus chaos, or wholeness versus fragmentation.

We will talk about trust versus insecurities, or understanding our inner reality.

We will talk about why Christ came. He came for you.

With all sincerity, at times you may think I am making random points and you may wonder where exactly we are going.

Together, we will be talking about everything from a party, to a garden city, to world geography, to personal and spiritual boundaries, to metaphysics, to what makes the framework for society, to daily life applications of said society, to finding influences on personal growth, to walking in complete alignment.

Just like a constellation made up of glowing individual stars, when the ancient peoples knew where a certain constellation in the sky was, they could conduct their navigation while at sea. And so, I trust, you will be able to find your navigation once we are finished pointing out the pinpointed stars in this "constellation."

With all the very best,

Lauren

Will you begin with me?

4

THE BUSINESS OF MINISTRY

In this chapter, we are going to regain the right perspectives. As I mentioned in the last chapter, we are actually going to shift your question as we start this process so that you can come to a more enjoyable and sincere solution for yourself. You have come to me with a question before reading this book: do I start a career in business or do I start a career in ministry? Remember the whiteboard exercise? Everything – except your gifts, dreams, and personal experiences – is first written on that whiteboard and then erased.

So, with only your gifts, dreams, and personal experiences left on the whiteboard, let's ask a slightly different question: why do I want to pursue this career? You may tell me, "Well, to show up as my best self in society." Alright. Well, let's make a jump, shall we? What is society? And what does a person's career choice have to do with society? Why would your career choice, and your career itself, either contribute or distract from the ultimate goal of being your best self as God would have it?

In the May 21, 2018, *New York Times* article, "Every Cell in Your Body Has the Same DNA. Except it Doesn't," Carl Zimmer presents the concept that both good and bad mutations within cells, once carried on as a cell "lineage," develop into what seems like permanent physical results. He presents varying examples, from the change of color in a fruit (that was not a man-made hybrid, but a natural phenomenon) to the development of leukemia or cancer. "It occurred to Dr. Walsh that he could use the mutations to reconstruct the cell lineages — to learn how they had originated." Could we use "[perception] mutations" to "reconstruct [perception] lineages," and "learn how such mutations originated?" Is it possible that entire lineages of persons have developed mutated perceptions of the significance of careers and of what those careers entail?

So to come back to plain speech. Where else do you find an extenuating decision-making dilemma in your life? If there is a conversation of indecision, say, regarding what restaurant to eat at, do you not ask *why* the question is being asked to begin with? If the why is only to impress, both an enjoyable and sincere choice may not always be the result. If the why is only to help or assist another's needs, both an enjoyable and sincere choice may also not always be the result. If the why is to honor all, both an enjoyable and sincere choice is most likely to ensue.

When it comes to career choice, you would like to have both the enjoyment of your choice and the refreshment of sincerity in your choice, yes?

Do you feel as if you do not know yourself? Let's start with the simple restaurant-deciding example: honor, not solely impressing or assisting, will probably result in an enjoyable and sincere choice for where to eat with whomever is involved. Honor. Honor whom? Honor what? Let's again start with the groundwork: honor the fact that Christ loves you. Honor the fact that you want to love Him in return. I am speaking, of course, in regard to your career choice. Let's dismantle this concept using Merriam-Webster's definition of the word "honor." If we honor our covenant with Christ, "accept as payment" the blood of the Lamb for everything in our life, "treat with admiration and respect" the Love which He bestows on us, and "give special recognition" to our placement of being grafted in the Vine (John 15:1-11), *then we will most probably find that the choices which grow out of this type of atmosphere are both enjoyable and sincere.*

THE PARTY

Let's say you are invited to a party that you are not expecting. You would gather information, such as what kind of party – a birthday, a retirement, an engagement, a holiday celebration – who is inviting you or who is hosting; who else is invited; what is the purpose of the party – is it a surprise child's party with the request for lots of child gifts, or is it a golden "50" with the request to donate to your favorite charity in the name of the person honored? Once you had gathered information (which is probably in the invitation), you would make a hypothesis about your placement at the party. Would you be looked for eagerly? Unnoticed but presence appreciated? Cheered on as you entered the door, greeted with hugs and kisses? Or maybe just accepted with the same politeness with which you were begrudgingly invited? There are many possibilities. You may think about what you would do if it was an outdoor barbecue, a poolside cocktail, a cruise ship gathering, or a coffee-shop gathering. You would think about conversations to be intentional about having, or perhaps persons to keep your distance from. You may choose to not go entirely, depending on the closeness of yourself and the person for whom the party is, or you may choose to make a quick stop by and give a kiss if there is a pressing meeting already scheduled for that date.

Or you may prepare generously and gratefully, with months of scheduling everything out of the way in advance, say if it is for your own retirement party or your daughter's first birthday.

The point is that all of these thoughts would probably flash through your head without you individually recognizing each thought, and you would probably make choices about your "place" at this party accordingly. Or you may deliberate a little bit longer and you might notice each thought, but once you had done so, you would still make your decisions based upon your beliefs about your "placement" at the said party. You would know your *placement* based upon the facts about the party. And, if your final choice was one of honor (honoring a higher priority previous engagement, honoring a close-friendship by being sure to not miss said friend's important party and so on), then the result of your choice will be one of enjoyment and sincerity.

The same is true for your career choice. And since we have already made the jump and asked, "How can you know what is your best self in society if you do not know what society exactly is?" then the same is true for society if you would like an enjoyable and sincere approach to God's perspectives. Many people believe the societies and nations around them are a certain way, so they determine their "placement" in said societies and nations accordingly.

For example, what if one viewed a society to be as so: the ground floor to represent all family, a wall to represent one's formal education, a wall to represent one's financial status or economic status, and finally a roof to represent one's physical health. Such a person would most likely be indifferent toward government, choose a career such as finance and become a financial advisor, and treat all family as if they may be walked on at any time because that is why they exist. Such a person will probably also consider poor physical health as the worst news one could receive in their view of how society functions. Such a person may also scoff at the arts and view language as a gift limited to purposes of formal education or financial gain only. They may come across to others as insincere because their view of what makes up a society is extremely limited.

But what if the original assessment of what makes up a society was incorrect? Then the purpose for why one makes choices, why one takes on certain attitudes, and why one's joys and fears are what they are would be entirely skewed as well, would they not?

What if the "facts" about societies and nations, as you currently perceive them, were actually a bit skewed, and so therefore the correct "placement" for yourself, as your best self, in said society could not be clearly determined? This is sadly the case for so many of us humans. We view the world and the earth as one way, we view societies and nations as another way, and we make our decisions about who we are and what we are to do and what we are to "bring" to this life in a completely skewed perspective.

Perhaps we have forgotten to honor God's perspective. To remember that He gave us the ultimate, undeserved honor: His life and His Love. You may think "never!" But many times, the blind spots are exactly where we do not suppose they would be. This is why they are blind spots....

You are loved. This is God's priority in realigning perspectives first and foremost.

THE GARDEN CITY

Life was never meant to be confusing. This is the second priority in regaining the right perspective. The plants and the animals and the elements do not wonder how to show up as their best self on the earth. God gives them breath and ecosystems and it all functions wonderfully without interference. Wonderfully. It is *wonder* that can, in fact, advance us. Wonder at all He has so graciously vested in us if we can only remember who we are with no interference. Perhaps God has given us breath and ecosystems so that we may function wonderfully without interference? Without interference of what? Without the interference of false perceptions of who we are, without the interference of what is without wonder; without the interference of what is without sincerity and enjoyment.

Today is New Year's Eve. A couple months ago, God gave me a picture (a vision) which I have not been able to shake since. I saw this sand dune city constructed in the midst of a huge desert. Because this sand was so far from any amount of water, there was thick mud being imported from many different countries so that the sand might stick together and so hold this city construction. There was actually quite the skyline for this sand and mud city. Yet a wind from the breath of God was let loose in swirls across this city, and all of the sand and mud was blown away, completely disappearing. But the skyline remained. There remaining, in the exact same shape as the sand city skyline, was a thick, brightly colored Garden City. It stood aged and mature, with all kinds of flowers and plants of every different kind of color and type, with vines and leaves and flower-heads standing in the same shape skyline as the sand city which had just been blown away. The Garden City had been quietly and beautifully and consistently growing from within the sand and the mud.

Immediately I got another image of small bits of grass or wildflowers growing through the concrete in a city, say like in Houston, Texas. The grass and wildflowers seem so tender and gentle, but with surprising strength and resilience, they just grow right through concrete and enjoy life. I felt God say that this is a message for our world right now. That across the earth there have been constructed societies and nations made of sand and mud, but the people who have gently and beautifully remained growing true to their God-given nature will be the societies and nations that remain.

Flowers only travel as seeds. After that, they grow, true to their unique flower-type, and never changing or asking to be a different plant or another flower or to not let their seeds blow everywhere else or to please remove all of this horrible concrete or manure or wherever they happened to sprout. What do I mean by saying that? When we allow who we are to erupt naturally as the timing and placement of God's atmosphere have designed it, we will not be concerned about where we are, where our seeds are going after they leave us, or how we shall become who we are meant to be. We will just enjoy all of the good in life and, with great resilience, withstand all of the bad in life. We will erupt from the circumstances around us naturally, honoring who we are meant to be, not who we may momentarily perceive ourselves to be. We will not try to impress or assist everyone who walks by, but by being the sincere and beautiful person we are meant to be, the people walking by who are looking for beauty will be honored, and the people walking by who are not looking for beauty will not see you. But that will not change who you are. Be like the flower growing through concrete.

You probably completely agree with me. And perhaps such a thought is nothing new to you. I am so glad!

WHAT IS HOLY?

The third priority in regaining the right perspective is to consider what is holy? What do you, you personally, experience as holy with your walk with God? Where has God (seemingly) randomly showed up and started speaking? What has been called holy already in the Scriptures? In Hebrew, the word *avodah* "jointly means work, worship, and service" (from the Institute for Faith, Work, and Economics website, the March 31, 2015 article *Avodah: What It Means to Live a Seamless Life of Work, Worship, and Service* by Austin Burkhart). In the gospels, Jesus uses the example of building one's life on the Rock, so that when storms come, houses stand. Is it possible the structures of society we raise do not stand because they are raised on foundations of (sand) skewed perspectives?

Why did Jesus come to this earth? To fulfill prophecies, to bring humankind back into a covenant relationship with the Father after we had broken it, to paint us a picture of what it is meant to be a holy living human being on this earth.

He did not tell his disciples to be in the synagogue four times a week. He told a radical fisherman to pay his taxes, and He gave him the money to do so.

He did not tell his disciples to act violently toward the Roman government as a way of fighting back against the oppression. He brought a government employee (a tax collector) to join his closest circle of friends.

Jesus did not pick his disciples based on their referral letters from the local rabbis, nor did he randomly seek persons and then surprisedly find out about their character later. Jesus was God, King, Priest,

Prophet, Savior, Lord, Servant, and all other names by which you have come to know Him. So, He already knew the character of Judas Iscariot. He picked him anyway. He already knew Judas would steal from the money he was put in charge of for their group. He chose him anyway.

Jesus was constantly realigning perspectives and giving new perspectives.

Even those who believed that He was indeed the prophesied Messiah misunderstood the prophecies and believed Jesus was going to overthrow the Roman government and become the King of the Jews, as they perceived such a title.

When Jesus made the statement, "Destroy this temple, and in three days I will rebuild it," people laughed at Him, perceiving that He meant a stone structure temple in Jerusalem. He was referring to His body. He basically was daring them to kill Him, saying He would come back to life anyway and actually fulfill the very purpose for why He came to earth as a human.

Jesus was constantly realigning perspectives and giving new perspectives. *He honored who He was, not who others perceived Him to be.*

Jesus spent eighteen years of His life doing carpentry, as taught by his human "father," Joseph.

Jesus made sure a wedding celebration had the best quality provision. And it was wine. He honored who He was, not who others perceived Him to be.

Jesus made people's minds, bodies, spirits, hearts

whole. He talked about personal relationships, public relationships, personal development, etc. He taught those around Him: "the Kingdom of God is within you."

He did not say please find the Kingdom of God, please create the Kingdom of God, or please tell everyone to come under the umbrella of the Kingdom of God so that we can protect them from the kingdom of evil. No. He said tell them that the Kingdom of Heaven is at hand. What is the Kingdom of Heaven? What is the Kingdom of God? I believe the Kingdom of Heaven ("Your will be done on earth as it is in Heaven") is where every human being functions as so: the Kingdom of God is within them.

So what is the Kingdom of God within a person? The Kingdom of God is an inner reality with its own culture, laws, celebrations, and all else that one might find in a kingdom. When this reality is given the ability to grow within us, we automatically welcome heaven on earth.

Perhaps you already know and appreciate everything which I have said. Perhaps you already live all of this out daily. Perhaps you just need to remember.

PROCESS OF REMEMBERING

Why do you do what you do? Why does anyone do what they do? Because they perceive societies and nations to be a certain way. They perceive business to play a certain role in society (good, bad, indifferent, and dynamic or set in stone); they perceive culture and art to play a certain role in society (good, bad, indifferent, and dynamic or set in stone); they perceive family to play a certain role in society (good, bad, indifferent, and dynamic or set in stone); they perceive lifelong learning to play a certain role in society (not at all, very much, or indifferent); they perceive government to play a certain role in society (good, bad, indifferent, and dynamic or set in stone); and they perceive wholeness to play a certain role in the growth or destruction or indifference of a society. And based upon perceptions, people make choices about who they want to be and why accordingly.

As you have read through this chapter, you may have noticed at times that you started to relax a little, or maybe at times a tensing feeling of condemnation would tell you that what I am saying is all lies and deceit, so to be on your guard. Conviction of the Holy Spirit is a "happy" feeling. If someone tells you stop, a train is about to hit you, and then you turn and nothing is there, you would probably feel confused, tense, and condemned. If someone tells you to stop because a train is about to hit you, and then you turn and the train just missed hitting you, you would be happy and relieved that the person told you. I hope you're starting to feel happy and relieved.

CHAPTER SUMMARY

- Shifting your question from: "which career choice should I take to be my best self?" to "why do I want to make this career choice?"
- Considering "I want to be my best self in society" cannot be truly realized without understanding "What makes up a society?"
- What is holy is the reality of the Kingdom of God within you and Christ being who He is meant to be, not who people perceive Him to be.
- What is enjoyable and sincere grows naturally out of honoring who we are, not who others perceive us to be. Let's make decisions accordingly.
- If we change our question, we can change our result.

Where to Start

- The next time a smaller decision does not come easily for you, try taking away all perceptions out of consideration and honoring who you are meant to be naturally. For example, you would like to choose an outfit for a meeting with someone, and you find yourself not knowing how to dress (not because you don't know how to, but because you can't decide). Try honoring who you are meant to be instead of trying to either assist or impress, and see if what you choose turns out refreshing and joyful to you.

5

REMEMBER WHO YOU ARE

"Your eyes saw my substance, being yet unformed. And in Your book they all were written, The days fashioned for me, When as yet there were none of them."

— PSALM 139:16, NKJV

God has put several large vestments in you. Remembering this is the key first step to our process together. He has given you many gifts. God says that He "causes everything to work together for the good of those who love God and are called according to his purpose for them" (Romans 8:28, NLT). This means that not only can He repay you twice for something that was either incurred or done negatively towards you, but that everything He has vested in you, He plans on seeing a profit of. He plans on seeing you enjoy your life to its fullest!

God has invested much into you (into each of us) – do you remember what He has put into you? Don't ever feel condemned for who you are if you find you have different set of gifts than those currently around you. Don't feel insecure for what others think of you because you are beyond their conceptualization of what is acceptable in their concept of their culture. Your skills are valuable – not just to assist or impress whoever is the most pressing person on your consciousness, but to sincerely enjoy the life that is before you! To honor the love given you by God. You are more than enough! You are as the "ugly duckling" in the children's storybook: you are not a duck at all, but a swan! And because of that, you are not recognized by many. Do not worry. The best is yet to come! You will "mature" and see even yourself for who you are as God created you to be: different, but good. And yes, you are different for a reason. We are each different for a reason.

You love learning. You appreciate learning. You appreciate other people or different ways of life. You appreciate other cultures. This is who you are. You are a cultured and educated woman. You have learned many things that have been proven in the natural realm.

You have received many experiences and learnings that are tools or gifts for accomplishing certain tasks at certain times. Those tools all accomplish one purpose. Building tools accomplish a building purpose.

Learning tools accomplish a learning purpose. Some tools have to be taught for new purposes. Whichever the case, let's look at the tools which you have been given.

I am sure you approach almost every situation with some level of the tool called "critical thinking," which includes the following steps: you approach a topic with no previous opinion, you run data and weigh results, and then form some sort of conclusive belief about the topic. I am sure you have applied this same principle within small and large groups of people – communicating about an issue with a positive outlook for a constructive conclusion, applying creative and innovative processes, and agreeing upon some solution to the situation discussed within the group. What a wonderful tool which so many do not even know how to pick up and use! If you can pick this tool up and use it, what a valuable gift! It can be put to good purpose at the appropriate time.

You care about your career's purpose or what your career's purpose will be. This is the purpose you have come to me wanting to accomplish. Perhaps if you had been non-educated and/or non-cultured, you might only make your career choice based upon capability ("I can do anything" at the height of this train of thought). But because you have seen and learned so much about many different persons and their conclusive purposes in the world around them, you care deeply about having an impactful purpose yourself, in a positive way, on everything and everyone around you.

I am sure you yourself have either traveled through other countries, come from other countries, or are planning to move to other countries. You are someone who can be resilient. You are a well-traveled person. You are someone who enjoys the expansiveness of life. You are someone who enjoys people from all different walks of life. What a gift! This is a tool you do not need to now acquire because it has already been made available to you.

As a follower of Christ, I am sure you have also followed the scientific method within your sphere of influence, maybe without even realizing it. I am sure you looked at some problem, gathered as much information regarding said question as you could, formed some sort of viable hypothesis, tested this hypothesis with varying choices, compared the ensuing results, and then developed some sort of theory about the original encapsulated question. This method is a tool. Oftentimes, this tool is used without conscious consideration that this is in fact the tool that is being used: the scientific method.

Perhaps you have been an avid history-reader. Perhaps you listen to the stories about persons and movement in the past, or about the way societies and nations were formed at their start. This method is also a tool. Perhaps you have compared varying accounts and decided upon your own more objective theory, or perhaps you have found enough varying sources from differing geographies and cultures – all with the same accounts of some historical event – and so you have come to believe that the evidence has pointed to you that this must be true. How interesting. What a gift those who have kept records have given to us! Such a valuable gift of observation for future comparisons – to be able to look through historical records (including ancient to modern literature whose content is indicative of the beliefs and situations surrounding the authors) and find common threads, geographical points, themes, and scientific evidence.

God has put into you certain traits that define who you are. He has put together all forms of ingredients for a final preparation of "you." Have you seen this with your own life? Do you see any common threads, continuing themes, specific geographical places, and scientific evidence to conclude a loving account about yourself? Perhaps you have already done this. If so, wonderful. Because all of which God has vested in you are tools to be used at some point in your life. No one uses all tools at once. No one holds ten different tools and tries to get a job done. They hold one tool, they get a job done. They lay down that tool. They pick up the next tool, and they get a job done. All tools are used to build one final house, or to learn one conclusive concept, or to serve one final purpose.

God has mixed all of your character traits and gifts and dreams and experiences into who you are. That

means your prophetic gifts, your real-estate development dreams, your experiences with mixed cultures,
your joy of learning, your desire to see both yourself
and others to be the best: these are all together inside
of you for a reason. They are the perfect recipe for who
you are meant to be and what you are meant to do.

PROCESS OF IMPLEMENTING

Practice the tool of critical thinking with observation
of history and geography and the scientific method.
Practice the tool of the scientific method with the tools
of critical thinking and historical reference and
geographical comparison. Compare historical evidence
through geography, the scientific method, and the tool
of critical thinking.

Let who you are be the first step to this process.

Why are we still not talking about finances? We will
get there.

CHAPTER SUMMARY

- Don't discredit any part of your life
  experience as being valuable.
- If you were given the opportunity to be
  surrounded by different cultures and to
  receive a great education, don't throw these
  gifts away as worthless. No, they are not the

answer to your deepest questions and desires as Jesus is, but they are wonderful tools for this life.

Where to Start

- Go to your whiteboard, which we have been including in our conversations, and write down everything that has been vested in you. Do you see these things as gifts? Why or why not?

- The next time you catch yourself discrediting part of your experience because people do not perceive it as valuable, excuse or detach yourself for a moment and ask yourself, "Why am I feeling these insecurities? Am I perceived as not worthy by others, or is that myself?" Whichever the answer, remind yourself that the only price tag for your worth is the blood of God. That is the only "number" floating around your identity: the priceless blood of God.

6

FOLLOW YOUR INTUITION

Let's put God's investment into us to work. In this chapter, we are discussing *how* you will be able to make your career choice. In the next chapter, Chapter 7, we will discuss the why. And as discussed previously, once the "why" is known, the "how" will come much easier. But first, we are going to "warm up the engine," discuss the how here, discuss the why (Chapter 7), and then prepare to "drive" in the right direction (Chapter 8).

A STORY

I would like to share a story.

During the time period while I was still re-learning to follow my intuition, shortly after my college years, I spent one particular summer tutoring a high school girl in writing.

At the time, I was very confident in being able to teach anyone. For some particular reason, I had no problem following my intuition almost completely during this tutoring. In a very "organic" way, I gathered materials I instinctively knew I would need to help take this student from point A to point B. I prepared a few exercises, tailoring what I wanted to do to a more specific ninth-grade level with some combined research added to my already previous experience. In addition, I prepared a few notes and outlines, interviewed her mother, and knew exactly how to proceed forward.

Even though I was hired to tutor a girl in the ninth grade solely to advance her writing skills, my intuition told me to employ very different methods. What the girl was lacking was not grammar or sentence-structure, but depth of communication – really transferring her heart into what she was going to say. I was asked to not only bring her writing skills up a notch to prepare her for tenth grade paper-writing assignments, but also to prepare her enough so that she felt adequate to take any college-prep test, such as the SAT, ACT, etc.

Over the course of roughly two and a half months, she and I worked on various exercises, only occasionally actually employing writing exercises. We did "meal prep" exercises for a dinner party for very specific, but imaginary, guests; we did some physical exercises with a beach ball (tossing it back and forth, comparing it to conversation); and we had conversations about the things she was reading and the things she enjoyed. Through these exercises, we were basically approaching communication through a more instinctive way and then adding the logic to organize the paper at the end.

When our time together was finished, I was surprised, happy, and excited for her. She was confident, came across as more talented because of the amount of depth she was sharing, and I hope she had retained some skillsets to take with her throughout her life.

Her mother was happy because her daughter's writing had improved, but the daughter and I had gone a completely different route than what was traditionally expected or considered "needed" for writing skill advancement (and this was probably over a decade ago, so please be gracious to my rusty writing skills now).

If you asked me back then how I knew what to do, I'd probably say I just did. It was instinct!

INSTINCT AND COMMON SENSE

So let's talk for a minute about this *instinct*. Or, more accurately, your intuition. One's heart and mind are often affected by (perhaps perceived) reality around us in certain ways. However, what does your belly tell you? Your spirit deep within?

If a person is dropped on an island with no civilization already there, what will they do if they are interested in survival? Start building shelter, figuring out food, and developing a rhythm for daily life in order to improve the quality of their life. If the island is small, they may think more about preservation and creating environments for better multiplying the plants and animals already living. They may become very sophisticated. Or they may not. But until their life is a little more steady, they will not worry about whether their previous traditions or ways of life are accepted here. They will not analyze things with opinions or worry how their heart feels about each topic. Because for right now, this person is probably following mostly their own intuition to survive, thrive, and develop some sense of steadiness. Perhaps this person has innovated some things that had never been done in exactly that same way before or has invented some new detail in regards to living a better lifestyle. But since they are on an island by themself, no one may ever know, and the only human who is most truly grateful is this person.

I would like to think of each person's intuition in this way. It is without any societal input, constraints, pulls, or persuasions. When I was approached to tutor the girl in high school, I was approached because the mother valued me as a person, and she seemed to firmly believe that I could deliver fantastic results. End of story. I wasn't approached because I had long list of abbreviated credentials or because I was part of an institution which was designated for the purpose of education. I was approached because of who I was. Because of this, I was given the complete freedom to follow my own intuition.

And when each person behaves according to their intuition, allowing their heart and mind to *assist* the intuition and not hinder it, then even society may grow into a better ecosystem for each and every individual. And when each person is behaving in accordance with their true self and raising up atmospheres for better societies, they will have more confidence to complete the tasks placed before them by their own decision-making.

When people follow their own intuition, they complete any task according to how they naturally approach and work through life (modus operandi). Oftentimes, when persons have one of their five senses inhibited for a season, they may opt to function more intuitively than they had before.

There are times when my intuition and comprehension at the time have disagreed. For example, with regards to literally taking time off of work and risking losing that very work (because the time off was not given) in order to refocus on my health. In some repeated uneasy moments, I followed what my mind was telling me, to focus on my finances and keep the work I enjoyed, and I ended up in confusion, insecurity, and even chaos within both my soul and my body. I became very ill. (And how do you think my finances were helped by that illness? Not very much, but I can tell you that I ended up with lots of time to refocus anyway! I should have listened to my instinct in the first place.)

It is as if one's spirit, upon being disregarded, tries to move its way up through your emotions and mind and even through your body to make itself known. The same is true for your emotions and logic – they will find ways to make themselves known if they are ignored incorrectly; however, if the intuition is always followed first, the emotions and mind will always catch up, resulting in peace and clarity throughout your entire being. I follow this "1, 2, 3" method whenever peace and clarity are not present in my life – first, what is my intuition saying; second, do my emotions agree and why or why not; and third, what does logic have to say *that can be added to what my intuition is already saying.*

There have also been persons I met who, after I have encouraged what their intuition was saying, started listening more to their intuition and became overall much better in almost every area of their life – their physical health, their career goals, their choice in what they allowed to emotionally affect them, their hobbies and interests, and so on.

Of course, one's intuition must be always followed. We cannot only occasionally do so. Sometimes circumstances of life can come with such devastation that we doubt ourselves and what God is speaking to our spirit. So we try to only use logic or only use our emotions to somehow find our way through new territory. But this will in fact only bring increased devastation, so we must focus on what the spirit is saying despite our circumstances.

I also like to think of intuition as the way a child who has grown up in a lovely home may operate. They just do things without wondering if their heart will be hurt or if their mind will encounter something that may stretch their current experience. In fact, children usually crave discovery, exploration, and new experiences. And they just are themselves. The very young ones will not sit and stare at the astronaut and the puppy and weigh the difficulties of choosing if they shall be a veterinarian or if they shall work at NASA. And if they talk to God about their choice, they will probably just laugh and boldly pick whatever they like. They will not feel condemned for not being a preacher! And if they picked a veterinarian because they like puppies, they will not feel any less intelligent because they did not choose to work for NASA!

Children in their natural state are not confused. God is not confused. He does not put things deep, deep within your spirit and then condemn you for following the very thing which He put there to begin with.

However, I have been in this position before, as I have mentioned, particularly in my twenties, so I know that sometimes as adults, we think God is just as frustrated about life as we are. Thankfully, He adores us. Does He get disappointed when we don't choose what's best for ourselves and others? Of course. But thankfully, He has many guardrails in place to help guide us as best as possible before we reach such a point.

HOPE IS INTUITIVE

Intuition flows instinctively with faith. Faith is the substance of the answer. "Faith is the substance of things hoped for" (Hebrews 11:1, KJV). When you confidently expect something, you can almost taste it, can you not? A hope for something gives a taste of that very thing. In some measure, we experience it already. When you hope to live through a very difficult situation and you have to move very quickly – say within seconds – you just do what instinctively comes. You still taste life, so you instinctively seek it. "If we hope for what we do not see, we wait for it with patience" (Romans 8:25, ESV). One way to paraphrase this is to say that if you are already expecting some desired result, you are willing to go through whatever process needed in order to receive that result. When one has hope in who God says one is, who God says each one is uniquely, then one with hope will go through whatever process is needed in order to receive the result. What about the verse, "Hope deferred makes the heart sick" (Proverbs 13:12, NASB). Hope set aside makes the heart sick. Hope pushed off makes the heart sick. Don't make your heart sick! I am talking to myself here also. Whenever I forget the things I am telling you in this book, I will talk to myself and tell myself to listen also. Set hope firmly in the deepest parts of you, letting it partner with intuition, and you will find that hope is quite intuitive. You will find new plans and purposes rising up within you, and that is good. Try them. They could be the roadmaps you were looking for. Even if some "roadblock" or "detour" turns out to be the very destiny you were searching for! God will use any and all means to help us achieve the best – to help us get the return on His investment ("Every good and perfect gift is from above, coming down from the Father of the heavenly lights, who does not change like shifting shadows" [James 1:17, NIV].)

Life is simple, despite everything that goes into making it beautiful. Life is not easy. Simple and easy are two different things. This is why hope is intuitive. Hope intuitively will seek out the most efficient for the most beautiful.

The topic of repression, or adult psychological disorders, almost always comes from either an intuition they rejected as a child or from a childlike intuition within them trying to raise its voice and seek attention but to which no attention is given. This can cause anxiety, panic, or outbursts of anger that seem to come out of nowhere. Usually, the intuition is very good about speaking up about harm being done to one's boundaries or about toxic situations which we must grow away from through our hope. "Hope does not disappoint." (Romans 5:5, NASB) "Through perseverance, character is obtained, and through character, hope is obtained." (Romans 5:4, my own paraphrase) Unfortunately – and this stings to myself as well – when people have lost all hope regarding a certain aspect of their life, it is often because they have not remained true to their character. Or maybe they have not yet achieved such character through persevering on the simple, but difficult, objective path through life.

FAITH ECOSYSTEMS

God's ecosystems (nature, our bodies, etc.) are neither sporadic nor static: they are wonderfully correlating and dynamic.

I am sure at some point, either in studying business or in learning about this earth which is ours to care for, you have encountered the concept of ecosystems. According to the definition found online at Oxford Languages, an ecosystem is "a biological community of organisms interacting with their physical environment." This concept shows up in the rebirth of forests after fires and the delicate but constantly resilient balance of animals, insects, plants, and elements that form a cycle of overall (big picture) benefit for all involved. I am sure we have all felt the effects of an imbalanced ecosystem either within a ministry, a corporation, a family, a city, or an entire world of nations. We don't see this in the natural world. Some lizard does not suddenly say, "I do not want to eat these insects." If it were to do so, than the ever-rapidly multiplying and destructive insects might destroy that whole ecosystem. In the same way, the plants do not suddenly say, "I do not want to breathe in carbon dioxide anymore. I would rather breathe in oxygen."

The point is: ecosystems exist for a reason. We should learn from them. If there is a problem, it is a problem with the system, not with who we were meant to be or with how we were meant to thrive. Am I saying something as one-dimensional as, "I am against organization"? No. In fact, I am saying the exact opposite. It is in fact a well-organized and thoroughly, but organically, thought-out structure that causes everyone to thrive at their best ability.

I want to address a variant of this topic. Faith ecosystems. Your intuition already functions within "faith ecosystems" naturally. Because your spirit is part of the entire spirit realm, it understands "faith ecosystems" while your brain has to be wired to help your spirit in this regard, instead of blocking it. Your brain is a tool, a muscle, a gift. It is an investment, and you can use it to multiply what your spirit already knows. This is also where "strongholds" come in – areas where faith ecosystems have been blocked.

We have already talked a little bit about ecosystems, and I am sure you have meditated often on the subject of faith or have immersed yourself in whatever God might be saying in order to increase your faith. You may say and declare things, you may pray the things

God wants to see, you may notice that your thoughts need to be changed and have worked on realigning your thought life with the love of God so that your faith life would be steadier.

Again, in order to understand faith ecosystems: "faith is the substance of things hoped for, the evidence of things not seen." (Hebrews 11:1, NKJV) Faith is a substance. Starting to sound beyond the realm of quantum physics? Faith is the evidence. Faith *is* the evidence, not faith starts the journey towards evidence. Faith *is* the evidence. We will address metaphysics a little more as the book goes on, but this verse essentially is a metaphysics lesson. There is a physicality to faith. It is a substance. Faith is the result of something, not the beginning of something. This is a key component in coming to a career choice decision. What is your faith the result of?

And now, I am sure you are starting to remember advanced teachings on time, and how time is actually more closely described as a marble than anything else. Those in the West sometimes still see time as a one-dimensional line, and those in the East sometimes still see time as a two-dimensional circle.

The reality is that time is more closely described to the human brain as a sphere. Hm. So, could it be that Faith is not a one-dimensional line with faith at point A and desired outcome at point B? Could it be that Faith is not a two-dimensional circle, with God giving us a dream, us receiving the dream, and then us living out the dream as a picture of the God who gave it to us in the first place?

Could it be that faith also, like time, is as a sphere? That our spirits, our intuitions, our inner persons, our innermost being is already keenly aware of all reality, because it lives in it, but that our hearts and minds and bodies oppose what our spirits already know to be true?

Was not this the good news? Was not this what Jesus said to His disciples? "The Kingdom of God is within you." And was not *this* the message that Christ asked His disciples to share: "The Kingdom of God is at hand?" Does the apostle Paul not share in Romans, in the first chapter, that "men (humans) *suppressed* the truth and so they were given over to a reprobate mind?" This is indeed amazing! When we push down the truth that is already deep within our spirits, our minds turn on us and become "reprobate." Wow.

This must mean that in order to be a whole person, spirit and soul and body, we must allow the process mentioned in Romans 1 to be reversed – we must reverse the process that ended in reprobate minds and "be transformed by the renewing of your mind" (Romans 12:2, NASB). Be *transformed* by the *renewing* (re-new-ing: become new again) of our minds! This is truly amazing. And this is a small example of a faith ecosystem. Multiple organisms have interacted with their environment for the overall benefit of the whole. Ah!

Are you starting to feel refreshed? Are you starting to have fresh hope? In the previous example, what we know about God and what we know about the world we live in were shown to actually be the substance of the same reality! No incongruencies so far. Innocent until proven guilty. And this, you will see, is the perspective change that we are moving into with this book. That the physical world not only affects the spiritual world, but that the physical world and the spiritual are actually made up of similar "stuff." Yes, the spiritual world and the physical world serve different purposes, and yes, when a person's spirit leaves, the person's body dies. However, just as the liver and the stomach serve different purposes within the human body, and just as a person could have a problem that started specifically within the liver, we can all agree that everything within the body serves one entire purpose, and that everything within the body is made up of similar attributes: blood, water, tissues, cells. The body works well when the body works together. The reality around us works well when it works together.

And this is how it is with society. It is in fact a well-organized and thoroughly, but organically, thought-out structure that causes everyone to thrive at their best ability. If we look at thriving ecosystems within nature, if we apply the same scientific methods and critical thinking which have allowed us the ability to improve both our quality of life and maintain a nurtured atmosphere, then we should have no problem in living within a society as a Christian and creating much more beautiful societies and nations. Did not Christ say, "I do not ask You to take them out of the world, but to keep them from the evil one" (John 17:15, NASB)?

Once we can compare what Christ has said about society with what we see already in the natural world and with differing proven methods, we will have no problem in knowing where and how our placement within society should be.

FULFILLING SCRIPTURE AND BREAKING MOLDS

Do you not remember that Jesus has said "I did not come to abolish the law, but to fulfill it?" This is another sphere example. Old Testament to New Testament is not a linear line, with everything in the Old Testament being just history or examples or precedents or the "wish that did not happen" part of human existence to God. No, the whole of scripture is as a sphere.

Again, this is an example where something is neither linear or circular, but a multi-dimensional and physical substance. The first half of the Bible and the second half of the Bible are not circular, with the ensuing belief that the circle looks like so: Christ was killed before start of time, time existed, Christ was killed, time ends, the circle is complete, finishing at the same point. No, the whole of this whole story is as a full sphere, with everything correlating to everything, as in all the dotted particles that make up a marble. If Jesus came preaching a "fuller" message than what the people were used to (i.e., hate is the same as murder, trying to figure out how to have adultery is as bad as having adultery, and the rules for abstaining from certain foods is usually for health reasons not just to have you not eat something). Jesus's words were always a *fuller* picture of what the old Hebraic law portrayed. The Hebraic rabbis were very stoic, strict, and hypocritical, by Jesus's own words! Jesus said things like, "I designated a day of rest and celebration for *you*. It was meant as a gift, not a choking curse." Okay, I did paraphrase that. He said, "the Sabbath was created for man, and not man for the Sabbath" (Mark 2:27, NKJV).

Jesus spent time with people the Jews never would: Samaritans, Romans, prostitutes turned Christ-follow-ers, tax-collectors turned Christ-followers, uneducated fisherman turned Christ-followers. Christ knew Truth (well one, because He is Truth) and so therefore He was able to be and act in the most truthful way.

So it is with society. There is a much fuller picture than many believe about this topic. Sometimes people either do not care or purposely avoid what is needed to raise up not only a livable society, but a lovely society. But if people knew that everything they did affected society and in turn society affected themselves – maybe more poignantly than they cared to think – do you not think that maybe they would stop to consider about what actually constitutes well-built societies and nations?

Perhaps people would then also seriously consider the subject of boundaries. Not just personal and inter-personal boundaries, but business boundaries, culture boundaries, learning boundaries, government boundaries, communication boundaries, family boundaries, and indeed what are the boundaries (proactive and reactive, yes or no, this or that, etc.) that make up a *whole* person? What exactly is a whole body, spirit, and soul?

Regarding breaking out of harmful or incorrect boundaries inflicted upon you as a result of others' false perceptions. The more you focus on only yourself – your gifts, your experiences, your development – basically being the best "flower" you can be, you will not have to worry about *how* to break through "concrete," because that will come more naturally (as in the "Garden City" example). So, if you work on your own personal boundaries for yourself (not trying to change the concrete or others who have determined certain things a long time ago), you will find you automatically know where and when and how to break through bad situations, bad environments, bad relationships, and so on.

Can someone's intuition be broken? Yes. Since your intuition lies with your spirit and one's spirit can be broken. A broken spirit feels unheard and without value. Perhaps other people stopped listening to you or put you down, perhaps you have gone through abuse, and then perhaps you have stopped listening to your own spirit, since no one else has listened to it either. Start listening to your spirit. Give your spirit value; give yourself value. God gives you value. God listens to your spirit. His Holy Spirit is always talking with your spirit. When your spirit is healthy again, your intuition will lead you along the path of His voice. Never suppress your spirit no matter who else may try to. You can remain gentle and smart in a dangerous situation, but never agree with the negative words or actions done against you. Speak loving and uplifting words to your spirit, and it will stay strong. Remember Stephen, who was stoned to death for preaching that Jesus was the Messiah? He remained gentle during the false abuse, but he disagreed entirely with what they were saying and doing (if you remember the account in Acts [Acts 7:54-60,], as Stephen was dying, he asked God to forgive his abusers.)

CHAPTER SUMMARY

- The intuition, in its purest state, is unaffected by the perceptions and strongholds around it. It functions efficiently (with hope) in the most fulfilling direction.
- Faith is neither linear nor circular, it is a multi-dimensional substance.

- Our spirits, our intuition, are most in touch with faith and hope. Our intuition will make the most faith-filled and hope-filled choice, so long as it is not broken.

Where to Start

- Keep your spirit healthy, and practice listening to your intuition throughout the day. You can start listening to the small things, if you prefer, and then move on to "weightier" items as your confidence in what is in your spirit grows.
- Try to follow the "1,2,3" method I mentioned in the chapter. Intuition needs to come first, then feelings and logic. Logic even grows from intuitive discovery.

7

INTEGRATING THE STUDIES

The studies are naturally integrated. When we see them as such, we can make better decisions, understand people better, understand purposes better, understand society better. When we can start to understand this key knowledge that all studies in their purest sense are made up of the same concepts, we will start to trust our intuition more.

As we have already discussed, our intuition naturally follows faith ecosystems. Intuition naturally seeks out what is hopeful. Intuition is well-acquainted with how to be objectively loving. "[Love] hopes all things" (1 Corinthians 13:7, NASB). When we let Christ fill us and fill us and fill us with His love, we will have hope. We will follow our intuition for the best possible result, even when all seems dark or cloudy or very opinionated all around us. Because "unselfish" love is objective.

And being objectively loving in all circumstances of

life will start to reveal all of the ways that every study in life is integrated intimately. One cannot say that an overarching theme for the successful continuation of a business is not at all related to an overarching theme for the successful continuation of a love relationship or the administration of government. And when one looks at the studies of cultural lifestyles, family, learning methods, communication methods, and government histories, one can see that concepts such as integrity, consistency, thriving ecosystems, abundance, and the appropriate administration of resources all contribute to having a positive impact on society.

So if we are concerned about the big picture purposes for our daily choices or our big life decisions such as career direction, learning to follow our intuition and learning to approach everything with objective love will bring about the most positively impacting results.

When we as humans can better come to all situations with love (and have no predetermined opinions), then we can better see and understand society. Faith cycles atmospheres and circumstances. Love raises up thriving societies (people and purposes of similar foundations) and tears down strongholds (a "stronghold" is nothing more than a purposeful disruption of a positive ecosystem).

When it comes to making a decision, such as, "why do I want to make this career choice?" (remember the question shifts from chapter 4), then an answer of "to love" will surely bring about a better choice than not. So then the question becomes, "What is love and how does it affect society?"

Love is the driving force of breath and life that all are given. There are several different types of love, but the love I am speaking of is the kind which says, "God is Love," and the kind as described in 1 Corinthians 13:1-13. This is the kind of love that raises up honesty, goodness, purity, and every right motive that no one could argue with.

Love can see foundations and commonalities in belief-systems that "build" societies. Love helps us to be objective and to see more clearly. Our spirits do indeed know how to love best, and when we follow our intuition, we will know that what needs to happen in any scenario is what is best.

NO PREDETERMINED OPINIONS

One example of love being objective and seeing clearly is the concept of "innocent until proven guilty," or having no predetermined opinions about a person, place, thing, or idea until a fully whole concept can be obtained regarding whatever is in question.

What is interesting is that Christ did not care about the opinions others had about Him. God has always been after our hearts, to let us be in an enjoyable relationship with Him for our benefit, but He has very strong boundaries. If people change their opinion

about Him, or if they have something against His character, He does not change Who He is. He just is
Himself. Why else do you think so many people
wanted to kill Him? Why do you think that the very
people who wanted to kill Him either loved and
followed Him at the beginning or loved and followed
Him at the end? Because most people are not willing to
keep their hypotheses through a process. Most people
would rather just change their hypothesis, instead of
testing varying options and comparing results.

But you are an educated woman. So I am sure you
have the patience and stamina to withhold your final
opinions until something has been finally proven
through various trials.

It is as the great principle: "innocent until proven
guilty." This is a remarkable and open-minded way of
approaching a positive way through life. Unfortunately, many would rather say "guilty until proven
innocent," as they violently oppose any person, thing,
or idea without having first made sure they had all the
conclusive and proven answers.

But you are not the many. You are part of the few.
This is why you are here, correct? You want to make a
difference in the world. You want to be an excellent
steward of all which God has given you. You would like
to give God one-hundred percent and be one-hundred
percent of the "you" which Jesus has called and God
has created.

Have you ever considered what is wise? What is

wisdom? If the Proverbs are compared with what Jesus says in the New Testament and with what we see of the persons given as examples is also taken into consideration, most likely a truly wise person would be considered either too "worldly" or too "radical" today, depending on what kind of church or group is being talked to.

I am sure Solomon, before his many wives, when he was just known as wise and wealthy, probably by today's Western Christians would be considered too philosophical/ logical or even wicked because he was wealthy. This is funny because he asked to be wise and God gave him both wisdom and wealth. It doesn't say the devil convinced Solomon to use his brain too much and then Solomon became greedy. But a lot of people will have the very same words come out of their mouth regarding the wise and wealthy today.

We can be passionate about something that is objectively (without predetermined opinion) true, e.g. investing in a certain stock will show a certain percentage profit between the hours of 1 p.m. and 3 p.m. eastern time. Alright, if the investment is put in and the profit comes out with the same percentage profit as told, then the time-based fact is now no longer opinion. For those two hours, in that way, with that percentage, it was a truth, not an opinion.

Of course, when it comes to things such as language (communication) – depictions of things to communicate (satirical cartoons, for example) or actions to communicate (movements such as women's suffrage) – it becomes increasingly more difficult for persons to restrain their vehemence on opinions, for speech and action are merely extensions of thought.

And without cultivation, humans' thoughts can tend to be very opinionated. But let us also approach communication with the lens of *no predetermined opinion*. Again, predetermined means you made up your mind before you had seen some sort of proven result.

One might be as young as seven and maybe had their parents killed by a drunk driver, and then when they got older, say by twelve, they may have studied drunk driving statistics, studied the psychology or medical evidence behind addictions, and then by fourteen, they become very passionate about preventing addiction to alcohol and preventing drunk-driving. Age does not matter when it comes to objectivity. Persons can have very great or very horrid experiences even at a young age and can find conclusive evidence while they are still younger than most adults. So, in this example, this fourteen-year-old may have the objective communication that drunk-driving does not produce positive results, is not consistent with good health, does not communicate anything beneficial (dead parents) no matter what you believe, is not a part of an organized life, was not chosen for a whole and undivided purpose, and so therefore is not with integrity. A child will follow their intuition, and as they get older, if they stay true to that same intuition, that child's heart and mind will expand upon what the intuition already told them instead of diminishing what the intuition told them.

OBJECTIVITY AND LOVE

Love says: "You were made in God's image. God planted His truth within you. Whether you suppress that truth or surrender to that truth and partner with it, you are still originally created to be an example of God himself. And if you were good enough for God to put breath into, then you are good enough for me to love, even if you yourself vehemently oppose me." That is "innocent until proven guilty," "hope does not disappoint" (Romans 5:5, NASB). Notice, the Scripture does not say people do not disappoint. On the contrary, all throughout Scripture, you see time and time again where God asks people why they are trusting other humans as more trustworthy than Himself. When we "hope for what we do not see, with perseverance we wait eagerly for it" (Romans 8:25, NASB).

This is why persons of great hope are able to withstand others continually bringing them down. Those with great hope can wait patiently for great results as they live out their lives with objectivity and love. God loves us no matter how we behave. But He would like to build with us too. And when we can be objective first, we can build with love and reach refreshing conclusions. Our decisions will be informed with wisdom. And our lives will show *to those who are also objective themselves* that we do indeed believe "innocent until proven guilty." And the wise will encourage the wise, and no one's predetermined opinion will be able to shake their identity.

Determining commonalities between studies (seeing the integration of physical studies) will keep you objective in your perceptions.

If we can determine what the common themes between studies that contribute to a loving, sustainable success are, then we can determine what will stand before we start, or as it is in process.

When one studies science and finds things *proven*, not accepted as a theory, not probably true, not "we don't know how else to define such-and-such," but truly proven – like gravity, the atmosphere, and weight – there are not two sides to the argument. Gravity and the earth's atmosphere just are not arguable. If you jump off a building, you will not float, you will fall. If you leave the earth's atmosphere, you will float forever on into eternity, unless you have some tethering device or great rescue.

I find that the topics which tend to be vehemently divisive for extended periods of time – say, for decades, or centuries – tend to be something not yet *proven* to people's minds. And that is fine if something is not proven yet to your mind. But don't be so ardent about a topic if there are people equally as vehement against you. Objectively study all data, consider all histories across all geographies and ages and genders, test the hypothesis *objectively* (with no predetermined opinion), compare all results, and see where any commonalities are. Where there are consistent commonalities over the historically-human-recorded-to-our-understanding millennia (roughly 6000 years), then it is probably something that those of us living in present-day time can relate to and probably accept as "innocent until proven guilty."

And if you have received a burning conviction regarding a topic – some pressing revelation that you cannot shake and that you must stand for and fight for, that can be also good. So long as you do not torture those who oppose you.

If someone believes the exact opposite from you, just live your truth and people may be convinced. Nelson Mandela was not exactly treated with dignity, respect, and acceptance for decades of his life. But he responded according to his truth with dignity, and people all over the world remember him for his forgiveness.

It is interesting to me how some people can so vehemently believe one item with points A, B, and C, but then completely oppose another item, *even though it still has the same points to it.*

For example, in business, integrity, ethics, communication, consistency, organization, useful purpose or some positive result or thanks are all proven across history, geography, age, gender, culture, and so on, to be needed for a business to maintain longevity. Of course quality of product or service and desirability of such can aid in short-term success, but in order for a business to have true longevity, the previously listed items must stand (integrity, communication, etc.).

However, it is interesting that, even though such things are proven in business, people in say, local governments, don't stop to think about the longevity of positive results by thinking about integrity, ethics, communication, consistency, organization, useful purpose, or some positive result or thanks. They just think the exact opposite, which is why "red tape," "bureaucracy," "who's who," politics, racism, laziness, disorganization, no communication, no useful purpose, and no positive result seem to be the points of vehement contention. Has anyone stopped to consider what actually has stood the test of time and place and persons?

How about art? The fine arts. The pieces of art or dance that have been admired across geography, across times, across ages, across genders, across cultures – those pieces. Can you think of some of them? The *Mona Lisa* for example. There is integrity (it is "whole and undivided throughout"), it is so far proven to have ethics, it communicates to all who view it, it is consistent to something which we cannot yet describe, there is an other-worldly organization to it, and it delivers the positive result of thanks to so many viewers.

This may seem simple, but let us continue.

Let us take an aspect of culture, say cloth-ing/dress/fashion. The Duchess Kate Middleton travels to various countries all over the world. Although in a few countries, she changes her style slightly (such as Pakistan, Russia, and places of extreme temperature or vary diverse beliefs), she is overall always of a similar look, one which no person across the globe could honestly say was harmful to them. Correct? Her clothing is of undivided purpose, it communicates always to the same purpose, it is organized for the same purpose, and it is used for positive effect as a way of saying thanks. She will probably be remembered and emulated for years to come because the way she dresses is received as a hope or a kindness, always with a purpose.

Alright, how about family? Across history, geogra-phy, science, where do you find psychologically sound results? Across all studies from the ancients until now, where do you find commonalities of *positive results*? Communication, consistency (consistency in character despite changing times), organization (for positive results, not for negative results), integrity, useful purpose (it is not harmful and is actually beneficial), ethics; the previous concepts in various forms produce the children who say they grew up in a good home and produce the spouses who say they had a good marriage.

HOPE AND LOVE

Let us talk about the subject of hope as it relates to determining commonalities between studies and objectivity in love. Have you ever noticed that those with much hope seem to be vastly interested in themes that aid all people in all aspects of society? People such as Viktor Frankl, Nelson Mandela, Martin Luther King, Jr., even those like Audrey Hepburn or Kate Middleton or Graham Cooke (I snuck that last name in for you to look him up). What about people such as Michael Beckwith, who speaks of "the universe is on our side," "life wants you to succeed," and "[the sanctified] ego wants both oneself and everyone else to achieve their true potential?" My goodness, these are very hope-filled statements.

Jesus does say, "I am the Way, the Truth, and the Life. No man comes to the Father, except through me" (John 14:6, NASB). So, if we are partnering with Jesus, we will know the way to go. If we are partnering with Jesus, we will know the truth about varying circumstances and choices. If we are partnering with Jesus, we will have life abundantly within us and overflowing out of us for the refreshing enjoyment of everyone and everything around us. Has any one human been completely, one-hundred percent partnered with Christ in all things at all times in all ways? No. I know I have not. And even the best and truest examples have not.

But the more we surrender to partnering with Jesus, not with persons and their ideas and their traditions and their opinions, we will actually find that we become more alive in all things, that we make better decisions in all things, and we become more *objective* and *hopeful* regarding our place in the world.

ARCHITECTURE, SOCIETY, AND THE REASON FOR DOING THINGS

Let's turn to the subject of physics and architecture. A brief summary of this study will include topics of such things as planes, lines, weights, levels, curves, supports, spaces, and gravity. A truly conscious and developed architect will consider all detailed items such as light and heat and correct placement of certain walls to best utilize nature's beauty and save energy. *Every building needs an appropriate framework and foundation* and all of the correct blueprint drawings to raise the construct up. There will be a need for the architect to know calculus, algebra, and perhaps even chemistry when it comes to materials and environment.

If all of this information and more is put into the raising up of one building, should it not follow that those humans who raise up their society should be fully aware of what is needed to raise up such society? Shouldn't persons be keenly interested in the appropriate foundation and framework for raising up a society? Even if one person's placement in society is to put plaster between beams, if they were careless and did something foolish to the building, don't you think they might care a little bit more if they knew that they themselves were going to be living in that building?

I know you care deeply about society. You are in ministry because of it. You feel the strong need to raise up societies in some way. You have this strong desire within you to see communities and cities and countries and families all functioning with truth, beauty, and strength. You want to see the love and truth of God growing through every individual. But maybe, dear reader, you have only seen it through lens of the consciousness that drives many Christian ministries in the West.

The consciousness I am speaking of goes like this: Are you familiar with the activity at the Texas rodeo where as many children as possible are signed up to run after several sheep in the hopes that one child will catch a sheep? I feel this is the consciousness behind the *active* ministries in the West (yes, I know, there are several "ministries" that are more or less just stagnant groups of people, but they are not to whom I'm referring at this point). It seems the overall conscious spirit behind Christian ministries is this very picture: *"On your marks, get set, go!"* And all the children run like crazy after the sheep, trying their hardest and best to catch one. And if they do catch one? They get a prize ribbon. And maybe some extra cotton candy from mom and dad.

But does this seem natural? Does this spring up within a person and burst forth simply because it is overflowing? When someone is called to something, it burns deep, deep within them and springs up and flows out naturally. Studying scriptures, including Jesus' ministry while here on earth, as compared to the Biblical message as a whole will show that God's method is never one of over-analyzation or overly-zealous heart-cries of forcefulness; His ways are also not without brilliant thought or without deep emotions. Everything is channeled by His Spirit, by His way. This is how He conducts Himself.

So, if you are starting to feel like maybe your intuition had been trying to tell you that there was so much more to how society is meant to function, what society is actually made of, and how Jesus and life and making money fits into all of it, well your intuition is probably on to something.

And maybe your heart even has started to already ache for a change of perception before reading this book. *Is this really all there is to reality?* Or maybe that is why your head is always spinning when you try to ask the Lord more specifics about your life's direction after you have been in the ministry for so long. Especially if you are already keenly aware of everyone else's perceptions of reality. Your brain has absorbed so much of other people's perceptions that you have begun to equate this culture with reality itself, and then you wonder why your experiences with God and why your experiences in the world do not seem congruent with your experiences within the ministry world.

It is because, for many ministry worlds in the West, reality has not set in yet. There. I said it.

Many of these persons have very wonderful intentions and are very sincere, but some, honestly, have no idea what they are doing. They are in a pen chasing sheep, trying to catch a sheep so that they can get a blue ribbon. Of course, some of these persons are not even good people with good intentions, but I am sure you are already well aware of those people and keep your distance. Or, if you have been that person yourself in the past, I am sure you spent many years working everything out with God (personal development) and let Him help you be a better person or closer to the version of who you really are.

PROPHECY (THE INTEGRATION OF SPIRITUAL STUDIES)

"Love is the fulfillment of the law" (Romans 13:10, NASB). "Do not think that I came to abolish the Law or the Prophets; I did not come to abolish but to fulfill" (Matthew 5:17, NASB).

So where does prophecy fit into everything we have shared? Prophecy is speaking the fulfillment of something. Whether the fulfillment of something that we do not yet realize in the physical realm or the fulfillment of something that we do not yet realize with our hearts or our minds. Prophecy is an integral part of faith ecosystems, where intuition and hope also "reside." Prophecy is meant to add momentum to faith ecosystems or to dislodge strongholds where the appropriate process of faith ecosystems has been blocked. Prophecy aids the intuition and hope within us.

So what is the why behind your career decision, *specifically?* It is for the creating of things that are not currently visible to the physical eye. It is for the speaking of things not currently heard to the physical ear. It is to honor what is not currently being honored in that most loving and objective way. In previous chapters, we discussed that when the *why* is generally to honor who we were meant to be, and generally to honor what God has already invested into us, then the results will be along the lines of what we are actually searching for. So how do we more specifically honor who we were meant to be and what God has already invested into us?

We can honor what God has invested into us and who we were meant to be by being that person specifically – the person He has prophesied to us and no one else – by knowing so deeply the reality around us that we can lovingly make decisions instead of throwing out opinions or living underneath other people's opinions or, worse, their condemnation or our own.

And this is where prophecy, or the speaking of things that are not yet visible to the physical eye, also comes in. This is how faith ecosystems can be encouraged and the intuitive hope within us can rise up. This is where leaders who have been given a dream, a vision, an account of a situation, can rise up and encourage others to follow their spirits, their intuition, their hope. This is where frameworks for how things should be built comes in, the framework for how situations should be raised up comes in. This is where those with special giftings to see and hear and know and feel what is going on in the faith ecosystems around them can act out of hope and make decisions in all areas of life according to the love that pours through them. This is where those who practice such gifts can set records straight by standing up for "innocent until proven guilty," which is to have no predetermined opinions and objectively come to a conclusion that will break "strongholds," those areas in people's perceptions that have disrupted faith ecosystems and stunted growth.

This is how we can specifically honor, or love, who we were meant to be. We can rise up prophetically, function intuitively, and be unshaken with the love within us. We can specifically encourage the faith ecosystem we are a part of by understanding frameworks and foundations in belief-systems and raising up societies accordingly.

At this point, you might be wondering: "How do I become well-paid once I make my career choice?" Follow the process to its fullness.

CHAPTER SUMMARY

- There are three ways we can specifically honor what God has invested into us and who we are meant to be: 1) make perspective choices based on objective love, and 2) understand how integrated all of life is, and 3) be the person who God prophetically says you are with no predetermined opinions as to what that looks like.
- We cannot say "I believe *x*" and "I believe *y*" if x and y are in disagreement with one another and do not integrate as a whole concept.
- Let love and prophecy propel you to new perceptions and a new lifestyle!

Where to Start:

- Look up Ken Honda, from Japan, and his teachings on "Money EQ." You may find his written book *Happy Money,* or you may find a shorter article about him or a masterclass with him. Do you notice how he speaks of how so many things in life affect just money and conversely how the one thing, money, can affect all of life? Can you start to see how so many things in your life can be affected by your "happy career choice" and how so many things may have inhibited it before now?

- Look at different geographical locations and see how varying societies perceive a business's purpose for society. Do the perceptions change in geographical locations? Do they stay the same? If they stay the same, what are these perceptions?

8

UNDERSTANDING SOCIETY

Now that we have discussed the metaphysics of basics in life and societies, I would like to discuss my favorite part of this book, and that is discussing the framework of society. As discussed previously, once someone knows how society exists, they can much more easily find their place and more easily commit to their purpose.

Perhaps you've read or learned about this in your studies. There are many different theories on the fabric of society. You may have heard about the seven-mountain concept, or slightly different, the seven-pillar concept. If not, I will give a brief summary. The seven-mountain concept says that society is made of seven mountains that need to be conquered. The mountains include religion, media, education, government, family, the arts, and business. The seven pillar concept, which I discovered others speak of with this phrase only recently, says that there are seven pillars which need to be raised, including religion, media, education, government, family, the arts, and business.

But for the purpose of this book, we have to put all previous ideas and beliefs – besides your own that have stuck with you your entire life – and put them on a white board, erase them, write new things on the whiteboard, let you discover and try them, and if they do not come with favorable results, you can erase them as well.

One such idea that we need to redefine and realign is the perception that the church or religion is a mountain or a pillar. Religion should be perceived as an organization or business form, a communication method, or one aspect of arts and culture: it is a monk in a temple, a concert with no curse words, or a nun teaching catechism. "Religion" is not a pillar of society. Following Christ is a foundational belief system, and there are varying nuances to different societies' foundations.

Let me start by saying that I grew up in rather extenuating circumstances, so while God and I made sure I was cultured, educated, sociable, athletic, etc., I did not come face-to-face with many church persons' beliefs and perceptions about society until I was in my twenties. By that time, God had already established several beliefs deep within me, as I had done my own studying and communicating with persons. When I encountered some "church world" beliefs, they rang a bell and even at times encouraged me to search for answers about life and society further.

Other beliefs, however, came across as a little shocking. Because God had been so close to me from a very young age, I always had His encouragement to broaden my mind, soften my heart, and listen to my intuition more. Honestly, I thought that anyone who professed to believe in God must be that way, and I was able to treat persons with compassion who did not view listening to one's spirit, expanding one's mind, and surrendering one's heart to what the spirit was already saying, because I just figured they did not have the foundation of believing in God, so how could they build the rest?

But then I realized there was a whole group of people in the West who claim to believe God and follow Christ, but then who carry a consciousness that having a low EQ is somehow more holy; that somehow to be observant, empathetic, and articulate was not valuable, and that to just charge ahead solely for the church group's mission without open-mindedly comparing the mission with the whole perception of Biblical scriptures was somehow honorable. That being imbalanced and close-minded to God's interpretation of His own scriptures is somehow more strong. I am embarrassed to say that I was so surrounded by such consciousness for so long that I ignored not only who I was but who God is and fell prey to such beliefs for a few years in my twenties. It led to increased confusion, decreased wholeness (which brings an inability to make quality decisions), and of course, a constant misunderstanding of the societies and nations around me (meaning every time I fell prey to such types of perceptions). It is emotionally intelligent to be observant, empathetic, articulate, balanced, and openminded ("10 Characteristics of Emotional Intelligence" from The Overture Group) to God's own perceptions of Himself. It is intuitive, or hopeful, and filled with faith to let God speak for Himself. Let Him speak however He wants to. His voice comes from a place of love, of raising up societies (raising up frameworks for living). When we listen to Him wholly, we will understand societies, we will understand ourselves, and we will know how to show up as our best self in society.

Looking back, I found that the person I was in my childhood, my most intuitive self from about eight to twelve, is almost near the same person who lives in my spirit now, except I have added more learning for my mind to multiply what my spirit knows, and I have gone through more experiences to soften my heart more to the world around me.

WHOLENESS OF PERSON, WHOLENESS OF PERCEPTION, WHOLENESS OF LIFE

This is what it means to reach adulthood as a whole person. Listen to your spirit, add learning for your mind to multiply what your spirit knows, and allow yourself to go through experiences to soften your heart to life around you. Some persons have remained broken until their deathbed and so never have fully experienced the adult person they were meant to be. Brokenness in the sense of being fragmented (your mind, your heart, and your spirit do not agree), not the emotional sense of grieving.

When one's spirit, soul (mind and heart), and body are not in agreement with each other, all kinds of horrible things develop. Thankfully, God is always there to gently guide and aid and love us back together, so He is not angry with us for being broken – only if we choose to stay broken after we are well aware of the problem. I mean, what loving parent is joyful when their child chooses to believe things that destroy their physical health and destroy their heart's responsiveness to any type of real objective communication? The only choice then is just to expect patiently (hope) that the child will intuitively "come to themselves" (which has historically happened) and allow themselves to go through a process for becoming whole.

This, in fact, is the purpose of ministry. Helping persons seeking wholeness become whole, stay whole, and become whole again if need be, as our human nature does tend to atrophy (death is final atrophy) – but it is up to us "to be transformed by their renewing of our minds" (Romans 12:2), allowing God to bring us from glory to glory – from one beautiful "level" to the next, forever expanding and multiplying our spirits as an encouragement to let others do so also (evidence of "fruit" if you are seeking Scriptural study [Matthew 7:16]).

Was not the first commandment "be fruitful and multiply?"

And if the physical and spiritual world are actually made of similar "stuff" (not just one material affecting the other material – but actually of similar substance within a faith ecosystem), would not that first commandment (or framework for an amazing life – remember *fullness* is the objective and sometimes things need to be said in certain ways for the human to navigate a much fuller being, God) actually mean that absolutely everything concerning us humans on this earth has the purpose to be fruitful and multiply? Our wholeness, our commerce, our family, our culture, our communication, our government, our learning.

We should build our foundations at this point of history with agreement as best we can with other points in history. We should build our foundations in this point of geography with agreement as best we can with what has proven true no matter what point of geography we find ourselves in. We should build our foundations with the best of what has proven to be true scientifically and metaphysically (there is not still some overriding contention – no one contends that the previous medical practice of blood-letting and using leeches is something to be believed today, and the ancients would not have believed such thing either –

this is why it is important to always look at the *whole*). When we build our foundations in relation to the whole, then truly we can begin to build a society.

SOCIETIES AND NATIONS

In the past few years, as I was considering why God and I went on what seemed to be a piece-by-piece journey through my growing up, it was almost as if God finally said to me, "Silly, please listen. These are all pieces of a whole." I got this image of an ancient Roman building with strong pillars constructing it. There were people walking within the building, admiring and enjoying it. This is society. A physically well-built construction for all to walk in and enjoy.

Some have specific tasks in having blueprints, some have specific tasks in bringing materials, some have specific tasks in actually raising up each pillar according to the building's blueprint, some have specific tasks of overseeing that all is done according to the blueprint, some have tasks of creating walls (if this particular structure needs a wall one side to guard from, say, blinding heat), and some may even have the task of painting all the pillars, or putting marble or carpets for safety on the floor.

But once the appropriate blueprint and the appropriate foundation is laid, and the entire group is building according to these two things, then the pillars may be raised for a truly enjoyable habitation.

Of course, what I am describing with physical terms, I am referring to as a metaphysical construct. A society is a group of persons who are going by a very specific blueprint of purpose with a very specific foundation of perception. A *nation* is a group of societies with *similar* blueprints and foundations. This is why a society could actually be made up of persons within several different geographical locations (and for those who are interested to learn more on the topic of time, in several different time locations); and why a *nation* could actually span across several different countries or one country might actually contain several parts of different nations within it.

"THE CHURCH" IS A NATION

"Built on the foundation of the apostles and prophets" (Ephesians 2:20, NASB). "Christ is the chief cornerstone" (Ephesians 2:20, NASB). "Upon this Rock, I will build my Church" (Matthew 16:18). These are all metaphysical statements which tie in beautifully with the first commandment, "Be fruitful and multiply." The Church is a *nation*. Why do you think all throughout the prophetic writings in Scripture, there are verses (phrases) such as "a *nation* you know not will come to you," or, "many *nations* will come to your light," or, "all nations will put their *hope* in You." These are groups of societies being referred to. One nation is made up of similar societies. One society is built with a very specific *blueprint* and a very specific *foundation.* The pillars of a society are raised according to these belief-systems.

This is why some societies are in shambles: maybe they never had a firm foundation, maybe some information was missing or even incorrect on the blueprint, or maybe some persons whose task it was to raise a certain pillar did not actually follow the blueprint, causing the roof to cave in.

There are several possibilities. And these are the hardest nations to rebuild, because all rubble of the crumbling or collapsed structure must be removed and everything cleaned and prepared to build fresh again. Of course, such societies can also be the most rewarding to work with, depending if there are truly positive results leading to thanks (gratitude is key for every result. Not everyone may be grateful for certain items, but those who actually live within a society *will be grateful if the society is constructed for everyone's mutual enjoyment*).

Of course, there are also whole empty, magnificent fields (metaphysically speaking of course) that need a society to be raised from the beginning. There are whole societies waiting to be raised with the correct foundation and blueprint and team of people working and enjoying together. There are many capable workers feeling pointless and purposeless wandering about without putting their hands to anything. That is fine. See if they would like to be "hired.". Or encourage them to find a team of which they could be a part – some society whose blueprint and foundation they identify with and who they feel they must help to build.

Do you remember in Chapter 7 where we discussed that the studies are integrated? That determining commonalities between different areas of life can actually help determine what is objectively true and what is not?

So this is how the pillars must be raised. According to a blueprint of gracious commonalities to allow a stable and beautiful structure. The wonderful paradox is that determining commonalities actually encourages a spirit of innovation. A common principle for each pillar (as is architecturally sound) that leads to favorable results will lead to a society standing firm and not being "blown away" like the sand and mud city as shared in the example of Chapter 4.

Again, since a society is a metaphysical concept, there can be multiple societies overlapping a city and there can be society placed in various cities around the globe, etc. This is why the Garden City as shared in the story in Chapter 4 can grow continuously and strong and be shown to have survived any sand or mud or blowing winds. Because it is referring to a framework of purposes built upon a foundation of beliefs.

THE SEVEN PILLARS OF SOCIETY

Let's talk about the pillars that make up a society. Previously, in chapter 1, I asked you erase all other perceptions and ideas except your own experiences and gifts off of your whiteboard (with the whiteboard representing your consciousness). The purpose was to clear your mind and to allow yourself to choose what you want to believe. In all of the previous chapters, I have tried to communicate various ways you can begin to build a skillset for determining what you believe and deciding from there what you are going to do about it.

So here, in this chapter, I am presenting a new perception, a perception about the framework of society. You can determine whether you believe it or not, and you can decide that if so, what you are going to do about it. If you are interested to hear a perception I would like to share, feel free to read on.

This perception grew out of my intuitive experiences and gifts with the purpose being to let God speak for Himself so that I could be better at decision-making, not just for myself, but also to help raise up nations according to objective love instead of any predetermined opinion. I didn't just want to show up as my best self in society, but I would like as many people as possible to do so in the almost seemingly "existential" sense of enjoying the fullness of Christ's love.

Throughout my life, God has taken me through

piece-by-piece type journeys. Remember how I said this book may feel like a constellation? The point is to connect the dots, find your navigation, and move in the desired direction accordingly. The stars or pinpointed journeys of my life were each periods of time where my prophetic gifts and intuitive dreams seemed to converge momentarily (for a few years) to show examples or certain aspects of life to be absolutely crucial for a blossoming society. I believe there is a framework blueprint for society that can be used for any loving and hopeful foundational belief-system, whatever the nuances. I believe this framework blueprint can be specified with the constructs needed and wanted for many varying societies and nations. This framework, or these pillars of society, is for the purpose of raising up society, not for hiding from it.

What were the stars on my journey of learning with God and various educational material?

Well, there was *government administration*. I was always fascinated by what constitutes a great government growing up and imagined speeches I would give to politicians as a preteen. In college, one of the numerous careers I considered going into was being a mediator with the UN.

There was *family*: what constitutes a healthy marriage, what makes a great wife – because I wanted to be one – what creates a healthy family unit, what is the purpose of a birth family or a created family?

There was *culture*. The fine arts was something I

spent countless hours on when I was younger, including lifestyles involving certain fashion types and crafts for daily assistance with living (such as pottery, cooking, furniture making), or designs of effective communication such as beautiful gardens or interior alignments and designs of beauty within a building.

There was *learning,* with all of its modes and methods and purposes across age-groups and other distinctive differences – all for the same desired positive effect or thankfulness (have you noticed, by the way, the increase in learning by so many in recent years? with everyone's "masterclass," various child education methods, and so on).

There was *commerce,* or business and finance. I remember playing a businesswoman as I was very young, and then finding the topic of "organizational leadership and design" a fascinating one as I got older. Finance, like for you, took me a little longer to dive into, but once I did, I tried to dive deep and apply anything that I learned. I actually came to enjoy this process.

There was *wholeness,* or the study of spirit, soul, body connection. Everything from stacks of psychology books, to psychological discussions with professors, to physical health's effects from a lack of wholeness, to every physical health topic I could think to immerse myself in. God actually started having me eat "paleo" about eight years before it ever became a commonly accepted and talked-about topic. I have had physical health issues to overcome throughout my life and one of the first things I learned – before I even reconsidered Scriptures on one's spirit affecting one's health or reconsidered learning more psychology to learn about one's heart and thoughts affecting one's health – was that I not only had several key nutrients missing from my body (specific amino acids from specific proteins) but that I also had several terrible food allergies! Bizarre as it may sound, no one ever asked me if I was having anaphylactic shock or if I was allergic to anything because up until around a decade ago, the nutrition and medical fields did not widely and openly discuss or address such issues. Suddenly, just a few years ago, almost everyone started discussing food allergies, missing nutrients, and putting into one's body exactly what your body needs and not putting in exactly what the body does not need.

Finally, there was *communication*, or languages, depictions, and actions for the purpose of communication. I was involved with so many different people and groups in college that I attempted to learn four new languages. As a child, I enjoyed the required one foreign language requirement for my education. As an adult, I tried to learn an additional three languages. I have yet to be extremely fluent in just one out of the eight I have tried to learn. I have learned to understand the basics of two, and I have learned to write basics of two, but besides that, I have a long way to go in speaking fluently at least one other language.

Of course, *communication* doesn't just include different types of languages, it includes *how* the language is used, *why* the language is used, and so on. Communication can include depictions, such as certain literature pieces or fine art pieces calling for certain social changes or pointing to certain metaphysical truths. Communication can include other depictions, such as satirical cartoons (previously in history often included in the realm of politics), or even just acts to communicate some extreme feeling or thought, like elaborate marriage proposals or walks for social justice, etc. Lastly communication can include actions, like abstaining from certain foods or businesses or being sure to invest your personal wallet in only specific items. All of these are examples of communication.

THE PURPOSE OF THE CHURCH

"The Kingdom of God is within you." "The Kingdom of Heaven is at hand." Think about these statements again. Meditate on them, consider them with everything discussed so far in this book along with everything you have personally experienced with God (aside from others' input – solely you and the Lord). Do you find any discrepancies? Innocent until proven guilty, remember. Don't forget the scientific method, items of critical thinking, and your history and geography comparisons. Also, remember the whiteboard.

Anything currently causing confusion is erased. Completely. During each new "trial" of perspective, as you are trying to find your footing as a whole person again, things can be written on the whiteboard, go through a process, and finally be erased if need be.

If you find within yourself no reason to erase it after you have gone through many processes with God the Father, Son, Holy Spirit, then add to your foundations and blueprints perspectives to be kept. Once you have enough agreed upon foundation and blueprint perspectives (you are starting to feel whole again with no incongruencies within your spirit and heart and mind and body fighting against each other again) then you are ready to join a group of people to raise a society, or even a nation, or even several nations.

But let's start with one society.

THE CHURCH AND THE FIVE-FOLD MINISTERS

I have always had a passion to see lovely societies raised up, as I am sure you do as well, but it was not until the beginning of last year that I realized that every journey God had taken me on was actually to prove a point about *a whole picture*. Ever since then, all of a sudden, all of the various dreams and experiences no longer seemed just for me to get my life in order and have hope, but for everyone. And so, in some way, I am hoping to now share, not just bits and pieces of things God has given to me (He gives each of us gifts by the way, as you are well aware by your own gifts glaring you in the face), but somewhat of a summary of the *whole picture for a specific purpose*: raising up societies that are well-built and enjoyable.

In fact, almost for my whole life, this has been a desire of mine. I just did not have words for it.

And, up until a handful of years ago, I had not decided on what direction to go in for myself, *or rather where my placement was* in society. When I finally started to have a whole picture some years ago, I was able to move in the direction of my correct placement and begin living my life as so.

And when finally I had the "ah-ha" moment last year that everything I had been through was actually trying to get me in the direction I was meant to go, suddenly I knew I had to share this with whoever would like to listen, so that maybe you can spend less time getting to the "ah-ha" moment and more time actually living in the "ah-ha" moment.

You have gifts. Not just business gifts, but metaphysical gifts. You have prophetic gifts. Was not that why you saw so many incongruencies between the ministry world and the business world and why you couldn't make up your mind? Isn't that why you had that sneaking feeling that reality was much fuller than many perceive? Maybe that is actually part of your calling. Maybe you are a blueprint creator. Maybe you are even someone who lays foundations.

Apostles lay foundations. Apostles at times carry the blueprints and then pass the blueprints on to Prophets to be interpreted, but often Prophets actually bring the blueprints to the foundation.

Apostles and Prophets lead the way for *where* and *how* and *why*.

Evangelists (and please those of you reading who are only familiar with televangelists or worse, some scam, please reconsider any final conclusions you may have made without searching for conclusive evidence – real evangelists are not like this at all, and *good* evangelists are the exact opposite. Reinhard Bonke is a great example. The gentlest and kindest person, with the heart of a child, but the authority of an adult man. What a great guy, in that respect) bring the workers who believe the same perspectives as the foundation and the blueprint present.

Pastors oversee all of the workers, making sure that they are working in alignment with the foundation and the blueprint.

Teachers bring in the paint for the pillars, the marble for the floor, the carpets for safety, etc. They are there to really help bring everything to life for everyone's enjoyment.

But without a solid foundation of integrating studies, determining commonalities, loving objectively, and following hope (the intuition or spirit inside of us), it does not matter how good the blueprint is, the pillars will not raise or will not last.

And without a good – no, *great* – blueprint on how to raise up the appropriate framework for a society, the very roof will cave in!

And unless all of the pillars are raised with the architecturally-sound method of following the blueprint and keeping in alignment with the physics of the building, the roof will also eventually either cave in, or not even "fit" with the pillars at all.

Finally, what is life without some real beauty added to the strength? Paint and flooring and safety measures that are also beautiful are also usually needed (usually, because sometimes the beauty of the material stands best as is. And yes, this is a metaphysical, or poetical [same thing] statement).

And some people may have more than one job or placement in society. Some people may have overlapping placements and callings, and that is fine. Because out of the seven pillars (government, communication, learning, commerce, culture, family, wholeness), which one can survive without the other?

This is another point. Each pillar, just as one architecturally depends on the other, so spirituality and physicality (same thing) depend on the other. This is wholeness. So, the prophet may come in with a blueprint, and then later assist with the painting of the pillars (this is where teachers and prophets may continue a closer relationship). Or the apostle, who laid the foundation, may then assist with the raising of a government pillar on that foundation by perhaps having several acquaintances who are in the senate and sitting in on several "think-tank" meetings, or similar. Sandi Krakowski is an interesting example in that, maybe without realizing it, she has laid a foundation for a belief system about life that many people have followed. She is also someone who has paved the way remarkably in several areas of business, teaching even those who the rest of us learn from on television.

BRINGING ALL CONCEPTS TOGETHER

Beloved, dear friend, life is so much fuller than many have perceived it to be. God "does not change like shifting shadows" (James 1:17, NIV). He is not swayed by the opinion of the time, or the opinion of the geography, or the opinion of a fact that has not yet been proven by science beyond contention (like gravity). He simply is. He is His truth, He lives His truth, He gives no apology for building His truth.

But He also never ever forces His hand. He always loves us and asks us to join Him in partnership if He thinks we may. He never forces anyone to build with Him, and He always, always, always builds for the benefit of everyone, whether they agree with Him or not. If He knows that something He will build will benefit some person who thinks that it will be detrimental to them, He may build it anyway so that person can be helped out of a desperate situation.

But He always builds what is beautiful and strong

and enjoyable and useful and for the giving of thanks in our hearts. He always wants to build so that our lives can be more full. He invites us to build with Him so that our lives will be more full. He encourages us to innovate, to sustain, to nurture, to preserve, *and to break where need be.* He has the healthiest boundaries, the most whole mindset, and the most hope-filled experience because He works *with* the Holy Spirit, not against it.

So beloved, your spirit is right. Your dreams are true. Let's put your gifts to good use and leave all else behind. The nations are waiting to be raised in beauty and strength, and we must all do this objectively (in love!) together.

You might be thinking: "You haven't talked about finances at all in this book. Why is this book called, *The Well-Paid Christian?*" Because believe or not, wealth comes and *stays* with the right mindsets. There is plenty of information available in the world on "money IQ," as Ken Honda refers to it. Ken Honda also talks about "money EQ," and how *perceptions* will bring about desired results in a very deep way. If one's entire life perception is lacking in EQ, wouldn't it follow that the entire life perception must be properly aligned, and then the detailed perceptions, such as money, can be intricately adjusted?

CHAPTER SUMMARY

- A society is a group of people who have the same belief-system for their foundation and the same purpose for their framework (or pillars). A nation is a group of similar societies. For example, people who follow Christ as an intrinsic way of life are a nation.

- A society is meant to be built by apostles, prophets, evangelists, pastors, teachers. An example of a prophetic leader who had a blueprint for the purpose of a society's framework was Martin Luther King, Jr. An example of an apostolic leader who had foundations of belief-systems to lay for many societies was the original namesake Martin Luther, who wrote the "95 Theses," which basically said Christ's acceptance was obtained through receiving Christ's grace, not trying to follow religious ceremonies.

- A society of any belief-system purpose must contain the following seven pillars to stand: wholeness (integral health), culture (the arts and how they affect lifestyles), communication, learning, government, family, commerce (business and finance).

- The nations are waiting to be raised in beauty and strength through objective love by those who establish belief-system foundations.

Where to Start

- Do you feel your "why do I want to make this career choice?" question has been answered? Great! Write it down. Do you know what direction you want to head in for your career? Great! Write it all down, as much as possible. Let it intuitively adjust, as you move forward. No predetermined opinions, remember? Begin to find purpose in the choice you just made. Hold yourself accountable. Be kind to your spirit. Let the Holy Spirit speak to you. Find individuals who do have similar foundations to yourself so that you can raise a society up graciously and naturally, not forcefully. Be objective in your love of everyone and be uniquely yourself.

9

THE CLOSEUP – WHOLENESS, COMMUNICATION, BUSINESS

I bet when you flipped ahead or read the chapters ahead of time, you thought this chapter was about something else. Maybe something else entirely. If you have learned or agreed with anything presented in this book, I hope it is these three things: holiness is making wholly loving decisions, your intuition (your spirit) must be listened to, and integrating all of life together will result in a natural and refreshingly joyful process.

WHOLENESS: CHILDLIKE OR CHILDISH

You have been given a map. Remember the discussion about the first chapter in Romans? All humankind have been given all truth already within them – *but not everyone surrenders to the intuitive hope within them.* Sometimes, people repress truth. Sometimes people do not multiply what they already know by partnering their heart and mind with their spirit, and walking as a whole person. This is a daily exercise for all of us actually, just as all of life is a daily exercise (or practice).

We have been taught that the child needs to grow up. And so the child does: emotionally and intellectually! Not spiritually.

Many times, this perception is actually reversed and people ignore the child in spiritual matters, and then tell adults that logic and feelings are not spiritual.... Wow. Jesus always encouraged an attitude of the following: "I say to you, whoever does not receive the kingdom of God like a child shall not enter it" (Mark 10:15, ESV). Well, if the Kingdom of God is within you, what is He saying? Unless you receive your spirit like a little child, you cannot enter into the fullness of who you were meant to be! This is what it means to be childlike: intuitive, hopeful, filled with wonder. The apostles shared, "When I was a child, I spoke as a child, I understood as a child, I thought as a child; but when I became a man, I put away childish things" (1 Corinthians 13;11, NKJV). What is being said? That *thinking,* or the mind and logic, must be constantly expanded upon. That what must be put away is *childish logic and understanding,* which is limited. Which is funny because, again, many church circles seem to encourage childish logic while at the same time saying "shush" to their children when it comes to spiritual, or hopefully intuitive, childlike topics. Again, the opposite should be true: we should encourage being childlike with our spirits, and discourage being childish with our minds.

And what about feelings or the heart? Not instinct, your emotions. Well, Scripture says clearly *both* that emotions can come from false perceptions ("the heart is deceitful above all things…who can understand it fully" [Jeremiah 17:9, AMP]) *and* that emotions are a gift from God (when in proper alignment): "Who satisfies your desires with good things, so that your youth is renewed like the eagles" (Psalm 103:5, NIV).

So, whether you have a blueprint, or many blueprints to share, or if you have foundations that you must lay, or if your hands burn to raise up and build a particular pillar, or to paint several pillars, *please* listen to your childlike intuition or your spirit and come join those who are of the same perspective.

And whether persons of the same perspective are half-way across the world or scattered across the country, please find them, either online, or even by changing your geographical location or by whatever means necessary.

Let's continue with this process of growing by talking about your gifts and dreams. Do you hear, smell, see, sense, and feel things that do not seem to be in the physical? And yet at the same time have dreams about very physical things, such as going into a real-estate development business or designing buildings or being a construction manager? Or any other beautiful dream in any other industry? An example of a few of my dreams happen to be in *business (commerce)* with real-estate development, in *culture* with building a fashion line, and in *communication* by writing at least one book.

Apply your gift to your dream. Use your prophetic gift to help see your dreams come to pass. Honestly, I used to not trust God and thought that using this gift would be taking a 'shortcut.' If my gift had been throwing a great football, however, and my dream was to be the best quarterback in the NFL, I would not have considered my gift as a 'shortcut', would I? No, I would have seen that 1+1=2. But since some gifts are not always perceived as being physically useful and physically beautiful, they are not always understood how to use. So if you have a prophetic gift and a business dream, *use your gift for your dream.* However, if you were someone who *had a business gift and, say, a teaching dream*, well then, use your business gift to develop that dream of teaching people. There are certain online personal development programs that come to mind for this example.

Or, if you had a teaching gift but an apostolic dream of laying foundations for tribes (as the slang word for people groups surrounding a foundation and blueprint today in the West is employed), then by all means, apply your gift to your dream and maybe start a webinar membership which lays the foundations for people. This would actually be ministry – empowering people to raise up societies by giving them strong foundations for changed perceptions with objective love on a daily basis. If you have a pastoral gift but dream of classic cars, go be an amazing general manager at the world's best classic car dealership or similar.

But since you, my dear, have a prophetic gift, and a business dream and a *society* dream, I will tell you two things: one, use your prophetic gift for the first dream and go into business if that is truly all you can dream about. *Two: if you repeatedly have dreams* also *about society, societies, nations, and people groups growing and raising up an enjoyable existence together*, then I would probably say that you are also a prophetic type of a leader. Because if you have blueprints running through your head all day, there is a foundation and a tribe waiting to meet with you. And some people feel weird about the word prophet. Okay fine. You are a leader. A leader receives blueprints and sees things falling into place as they should be and wants to raise up societies and nations (or even just one society) based upon that blueprint. Do you remember Martin Luther King, Jr.'s speech, "I have a dream…?" He had a vision for societies to be functioning in all areas of life with racial equality. He wanted to see every aspect of societies functioning with the common strength that uses objective love and not predetermined opinions. He rose up with others as a Garden City, peaceful and intelligent and persevering through the sand and mud, and raised up several people who followed this blueprint. Isn't that amazing?

So, my dear, you are probably a leader – be it a leader of a small group of people around a slight change of perspective in society or a leader with a vision for lots of perspective change for lots of different societies to grow all over the world.

Be both. Be a leader, go into business, live your dreams, and use that prophetic gift with objective love, intuitive hope, physical faith and with all the congruency of Scriptures taken as a full, whole picture.

And if you have many gifts and many dreams, well, roll-up your sleeves, you have a lot of work to enjoy ahead of you.

So, let's look at what a wholeness pillar, or a whole person, might look like. Then, we can look at what a communications pillar might look like. Lastly, for this book, we look at what a business and finance pillar might look like.

Maybe someday I – or someone else – can go into more depth (there is so much to talk about and learn for all of us!) for all seven pillars, but for now I'll focus on the mentioned three.

WHOLENESS PILLAR

Or as the Hebrew word *shalom* signifies, "nothing missing, nothing lacking, nothing broken." The wholeness pillar might be based on the following four big principles: the raising up movement might be based on the concept of *your individual spirit*; the pressing down might be the concept of partnering with the *Holy Spirit*; the turning left might be the concept of one's body, or *physical health*; and the turning right might be the concept of one's soul, or *the mind and the heart* (which can sometimes be described as "the will" – the heart is the seat of the will, and the mind is the crown of the will – meaning your will to do something is simply either a partnering with your spirit and God's spirit with your body, or it is not).

COMMUNICATION PILLAR

Languages – through both speech and body – and depictions – giving of images such as a television clip, giving of poetry, receiving of a song, and actions – make up the communication pillar. These are examples. But I hope it gets you thinking and expanding, and hopefully something along the way will stir up hope deep within you, whether you agree with what I have said or not and whether you have more to add to the conversation or not. But to return to communications. This pillar might be constructed of the following four principles: the raising up concept might be *a desired action from the receiver of this communication*; the pressing down concept might be *method of communication*; the turning left concept might be *outgoing commu-*

nication; and the turning right concept might be *incoming information.*

BUSINESS (COMMERCE) PILLAR

For a brief moment, we will talk about metaphysics, or the physicality of spiritual items.

A pillar (if you were a potter creating a model stadium piece with seven pillars) has four basic movements to construct its shape. You have the pulling up, the pressing down, the turning right, and the turning left. The pulling up might be a concept such as *giving a congruent and positive consciousness*, or, what is sometimes defined as, "creating the right business culture/value-system," but as a Christian, what you might define as "filling the atmosphere with praises." However you might define it, the concept still basically is giving a congruent and positive consciousness. The pressing down might be to *receive presence*, or to be open-minded/objective/soft-hearted/loving towards the whole purpose and provision for the pillar. The turning left might be a concept such as having the right relationships, or *giving authority* to someone by allowing them to create a business transaction with you. The turning right might be a concept such as *having integrity in all transactions* or receiving other persons voices into the creation and sustaining of the business (you might receive people's voices by conducting market research to conclude what the customer wants or by receiving input from a business partner, etc.).

These are four big principles, and then the entirety of the pillar could then be further defined by more detailed concepts underneath these four starting principles.

CHAPTER SUMMARY

- One aspect of wholeness is to be childlike in spirit, not childish in thought.
- Another aspect of wholeness as a person is to apply your gifts to your dreams, whatever your gifts or whatever your dreams. Do you have dreams of a "white-picket fence" family and an amazing gift in athletics? Okay, apply your gift with everything in you, and that white picket fence family will probably be possible. Do not apply your dreams to your gifts. We don't have time to go into the discussion here, but it will cause much confusion in your life, as I am sure you have experienced if you have tried to do this already.
- Every aspect of society should be constructed with whole purpose, according to the framework design of that particular whole society.

Where to Start

- Go through the "Process" sections at the end of each chapter up until now, and see if anything new springs up out of you. New perceptions are built with the processes of growing, changing, implementing, testing, and remembering.

- Apply your gifts to your dreams, make your detailed decision plan for your career choice with the Lord and your intuition. I know, with your brilliance, you will be a well-paid Christian with firm convictions and a multiplying lifestyle.

10

WHO TO FOLLOW – FINDING INSPIRATION

How are you feeling? Do you need a long bath while you think everything over? Do you feel the urge to go on a two-week vacation to reassess your entire life? Do you feel excited to explore new things on your whiteboard in new ways? Have you felt completely repulsed by what you have read here? No matter your response, I hope dearly that it encourages you to stand firm in your convictions about life and reality.

Of course, I mostly hope that you are intrigued, and perhaps excited, to live a fuller and more refreshing life.

So if you are still on track with me and you have liked what you read so far, let's continue.

In this chapter, we will discuss a much more fun topic than solely philosophical perceptions for a more abundant existence. No, in this chapter, we will get to play a little bit.

So, how is your memory concerning most of the things so far? Do you need to flip a few pages back? Maybe take a peek back much further than that? Feel free to do so. Here, we are going to find new inspirations for you. If you like what you hear regarding the framework of society and the desire of God to see us raise up societies by following our intuition, than it is time to find some new mentors. What do I mean? Well, where did you get all other perceptions before? If they were perceptions acquired from others without your own input, then it is not really your perception, is it? Be yourself. Be beautiful.

Do you see a tree? How about a large, sprawling oak tree that has been alive for a couple centuries? Let's say every branch is someone who you look up to regarding some aspect of society, and you would like to apply it to your own life. (If you can think of no one in that spot, describe who someone there might look like.) You can list multiple persons for one pillar and one person for another pillar, or you can even have a person whose foundation you align with, etc.

At the base of the tree is you, waiting to absorb all that you can and grow out with your own branches for others.

Or, you can do this as a simple drawing. You can draw a trunk of the tree, where those whose foundations you align with (or the foundations you have to give, if you are an apostle) are named, you can draw a root system with leaders (as described earlier in the book) or prophets whose blueprints you align with (or you can write out some of your own blueprints, if you have been given blueprints to give others), and lastly you can draw branches where each of the seven pillars is represented with someone whose perceptions you align with regarding one of the seven pillars.

Then, you can mix and match and go join, *or better yet be a part of the raising up of,* a society, then several societies, nations, and as broad as God leads your spirit. "He also brought me out into a broad place…." (Psalm 18:19, NKJV). "The land you have given me is a pleasant land. What a wonderful inheritance!" (Psalm 16:6, NLT). These are a couple of Scriptures to think extensively on in regards to persons throughout history, across geographies, and using the comparisons of critical thinking, scientific method, etc.

For example, I have Scriptures (the Bible as modern persons call it) as the biggest part of the tree trunk for my mentorship. However, I also have some persons from the company Mindvalley at my side in this drawing, as their foundations aligned with what my spirit wanted to build on. I have Kenneth Copeland and his talks on faith in all aspects of society as part of the tree trunk (which for this exercise represents foundations). All three of these listed I choose to learn from only where there are congruencies. Of course, since I have committed my life to Christ, I seek to understand the

Scriptures for everything – foundations, blueprints, pillars, and all details – but the point is to find out for yourself what proves to be true. For myself, Christ has never been proven "guilty" ("innocent until proven guilty," remember), while other life-defining truths have actually had great incongruencies to me personally from my own studies and comparisons as shared with the methods in this book. Christ has been very real to me.

And Christ is very real to you! This is why you have probably picked up this book in the first place! You wanted to know which direction to go in your life to earn money, and you love Jesus.

So let's get back on track, shall we?

Alright, the tree drawing exercise and finding inspirations.

To continue: for my example, I have Duchess Kate Middleton and some architecture and interior design and fashion persons for the pillar of Culture written on one tree branch. I also have famous ballet listed on this branch.

For the pillar of Business/Commerce, I have Ms. Sandi Krakowski and some of my own perspective on organizational leadership and design written down on a tree branch. Since most athletes are paid and paid well during this time, you may take example yourself from a particular athlete. Or you may see a particular sport as an art, say like golf, and put it under the category for Culture. Or, you may even see a sport, like

Olympic running, as a communication, or something very poetic that gives you inspiration for life. Wonderful. List it under Communication.

For the Communication pillar, I have travel, Scripture, and learning languages written down on a tree branch, as I feel these things lead to more objective communication with more intuitive hope.

For the Government administration pillar, I have written a few names and some of my own perspectives on the administration of a country for the purpose of raising up societies. I have included certain concepts of proper alignment, as I feel it is necessary to understand this in Government, even if you describe this sort of concept with different words.

For the Wholeness pillar, I have written on a tree branch Mr. Graham Cooke, being in nature, "holistic" health preventatives and remedies, the continual application of personal boundaries, and Scripture. You might have sports or something that encourages you to be connected as spirit soul body.

For the Learning pillar, I have written on a tree branch that "forever learning" is a must and that varying structures and modules are necessary.

For the root system, or for the actual blueprint for a society and why each of these persons mentioned are a part of my belief for how each pillar should be raised, that is taken from all of my notes throughout the years. Notes big enough for another book. I have always seen myself as a leader, but I just didn't know when I would reach the maturity to be in that placement for some societies for a time (even if that placement is a more hidden, or less recognizable one). So, for you, if you are also a leader and you already have blueprints in your head, by all means, use your prophetic gift and draft the blueprints. Just be sure to apply some process such as the one in this book, or some comparable way to prove congruencies and objective love in what you are drafting.

Now, of course, these are just a few examples of the people I found certain levels of alignment with. They do not endorse me or this book in any way, but I wanted to share these references with you in case you want to seek them out for yourself.

Are these all persons with whom I am completely on board? No.

That is why, in order to build what I perceive as congruent for the types of societies I would like to build, I have only taken bits and pieces of what resonates most.

Do the persons I have listed change at times? For sure. Again, this is just an example.

Some of the persons I listed may be building different types of societies or even nations than I aspire to be a part of. Some of the persons I listed may be within a nation I am apart of building, but not within the same society. That is fine. I am focused on being the unique creation I am and being a part of the unique society, societies, nation, and nations I am meant to be a part of.

Just like with the Garden City story, you notice it wasn't the Live Oak City or the Long Stem Rose Hybrid City. No, it was a garden. Be you. Be beautiful. Be unique. Be *whole.* If you are whole and you allow yourself to expand and you apply yourself to learning about what actually makes up a society, you will not only aid in raising up society, but you will be exactly where you are meant to be.

Now it is your turn.

Why a tree, when the whole framework for a society has been portrayed as a pillared stadium from Roman times?

Just to get you thinking organically.

If you already are thinking in that way, or if you would like to come up with your own exercise or even draw out a seven-pillared stadium building with a foundation and a corresponding blueprint, and you would like to find your inspirations and write them directly in this way, that is great also.

I just used the tree because I can get stuck in my left brain, so I try to do exercises to get myself thinking more organically, but perhaps that is no problem for you when it comes to brainstorming in this way.

And this is just an exercise to help move you forward into increasingly more expanding perceptions. Follow your intuition. Let your heart and mind partner and multiply. Bear fruit. Enjoy.

11

NOTHING IS LACKING – PEACE

According to the Online Etymology Dictionary, the Jewish word of greeting "shalom" literally means "peace," and properly means "completeness, soundness, welfare," (from the root of shalam: "was intact, was complete, was in good health").

Are you familiar with tuning forks? It is a two-pronged large metal object created (I believe) with certain densities so that the sound upon hitting the prongs is a specific musical note. If a musical instrument is not quite "in tune," then the sound of the fork can help while tuning the instrument. I believe the tuning fork is also used for the voice in assisting the voice to be in tune with the correct note.

When the tuning fork is touched and stilled, the sound ceases.

Are you ready for the constant vibrating noise of

confusion to cease? Has it already begun to cease with only occasional "flare-ups?" Would you like to be touched by the Holy Spirit and stilled, so that the atmosphere within and surrounding you is peace?

This requires a surrender. A conscious quieting of our own mind, our own heart, and at times even a complete stillness of our body. As we inhale deeply and exhale deeply, aware of only the stillness, we can at last listen.

We can hear God's spirit speaking to our spirit.

For a couple years after the first time I really experienced an immense breakthrough in stillness in (I believe) 2015 (God's presence was like a thick blanket, and it was as if He rewrote all of my past to be just how I had wanted), I still was not completely decided about my placement in society because I was still undecided about my perspective on society itself. I had spent about seven years around people in various "ministry worlds" in both the Western hemisphere and Eastern hemisphere (from about 2005 to 2017, with a couple pauses in between). And honestly, because they were the first other Christians I had met, it was as if I was a tuning fork that had been hit, and I was continuously vibrating with my mind and heart making noise and fighting what my spirit was saying.

There were a few people I met also during this time who had quite congruent and loving perspectives with no predetermined opinions. Unfortunately, I made the mistake of not truly investing myself with their acquaintance or friendship, and I chose the easier friends to make at the time. A few years after losing that opportunity, I became acquainted with some other persons, this time not in person but through some books or the internet. I had learned a little since my previous passed opportunity, so I invested myself into what they had to say. But I did not continue to expand and find others and truly invest in my own stillness.

It was not until I joined a Spanish-speaking congregation for about eight months and immersed myself into their world that I had this encounter of immense stillness with God. It happened not once, not twice, but at least three times. For hours. What was different? For the first time, I felt as if my spirit had been almost recognized. What else was different? People were grateful about every little thing with their business. People were trying to put back together their broken families instead of avoiding the issues. There was always a celebration with well-prepared cooking or dancing or something that was sharing joy. They always seemed ready to learn whatever they could with a grateful heart. With what seemed sincere intention, these people were trying to figure what foundation to lay down, what blueprint to develop, and were trying to raise one pillar at a time.

Now, of course, they were not thinking that way, it was a little more natural and organic, but it was the first time I had seen a group of people who believed Christ and who chose to invest in stillness and who tried, on some level, to raise up some semblance of life and living. It was not at all like any other group I had been a part of, and I had been a part of all kinds of ministry groups with so many different nationalities and even parts of the world. I think most of the groups I had been a part of were influenced in some way or another by this kind of awkward perception that being Christian means you are cut off from the world. Jesus prayed, "[My greatest wish] is not that you would take them out of the world, but that you would protect them from the evil one" (John 17:15, my own paraphrase). Later, one of the apostles wrote "we are in the world, but not of the world." We are meant to be as the Garden City, growing up beautifully and uniquely and peacefully, but not without notice, as the sand and mud are blown away. "The Kingdom of God is within you." "The Kingdom of Heaven is at hand."

From 2015 to 2017, it was if I was remembering everything I had learned alone with God up until 2005. Then, in 2017, I was provided some opportunities to begin my first real-estate investment and development projects, and from then until now I have been able to slowly increase and expand by applying my gifts to my dreams and allowing my spirit to take charge because it knows how to follow God best.

Has everything just all happened in the blink of an eye? No. But I am satisfied with my placement (where I belong in raising up societies).

And I no longer wonder how I am going to both

"make money and do what I am passionate about and satisfy my dreams." It is not even a thought anymore. Is work difficult? Sure. Is life difficult? Sure. Is daily life a consistent practice of being still and expanding? Yes. Am I satisfied with reaching all of my dreams already? No. Because I have not! But I am excited about my choices every day. I know the results will come because I have taken my place, and already I have seen results trickle in gladly for the past few years. The best is yet to come. And it will for you too.

Where to Start

- Practice being still (the tuning fork example). Do not let anyone else tune you but the Holy Spirit. He will guide you into all truth.
- Practice expanding your intuition by applying your expanding heart and your expanding wisdom to your ever-stilled intuition (like the tuning fork).

BUILDING TOGETHER WITH OUR
KING AND PRIEST

I know how difficult it is to find the right answer. There are plenty of answers, but which ones will actually help? Which ones will actually save time not waste time? You have dreams, and you have big dreams. You have compassion for people. You have every desire to shift societies, to shape societies. You see things, hear things, feel things, sense things, smell things. Some hear mighty words which sound beautiful and majestic at first, but the interpretations of which seem to leave you feeling dry crumbs in your mouth. Are some interpretations actually missing the mark?

You see buildings. Buildings that aren't there yet.

You dream social movements. You have a deep longing within you – you wish you could see the final results now!

And the biggest question that bothers you – why haven't you figured it out already? God seems to delight in telling and showing you everything else – why not simply telling and showing what choice you are to make for your life's purpose?

Or maybe He already has?

In this book, we discussed how I have been in a very similar situation. How I was disappointed, wondering how to put all of the puzzle pieces together, and feeling I needed to speak and be heard.

In this book, we discussed how, since you are cultured and educated, you probably already have some key knowledge regarding history, science, thinking skills, and the different cultures geographically around the world.

In this book, we also continued with the concepts of instinct and common sense, touching on physics and architecture and faith ecosystems.

We discussed consistency, communication, organization, integrity, and purposes creating effects of gratitude when determining similar constructions among different items in society; how the studies are integrated and hope is intuitive.

We discussed having no predetermined opinions at first and reaching conclusions of objective love after comparing results.

These are our foundations.

For a very general, wide-focus, sketch of a blueprint, we simple discussed the basics of a framework for society. We discussed the seven pillars to be raised in each society: wholeness, government, family, business or commerce, culture, learning, and communication.

We talked of societies making up nations. We talked about belief-systems and frameworks for living as being what makes up a society.

As we dove in deeper to look at daily applications of raising a society, we specifically looked at three pillars: business/ commerce (integrity, atmosphere, relationships, transactions), wholeness (your spirit, God's spirit, your soul, your body), and communications (languages, depictions, actions, methods, information, outcomes).

As we pulled our process to a close, we talked about what inspires you and we worked through some examples together.

Throughout this book, we talked about "be fruitful and multiply," and how we can be still, listen to our spirit, and then apply our heart and mind to the multiplication of what our spirit is already saying.

Throughout this book, we also discussed Christ's words of "The Kingdom of God is within you," and "The Kingdom of Heaven is at hand."

God wants us to be in right alignment, God wants us to be at peace. He wants us to still all other voices so that only our spirit and His spirit can be heard. Then, we can study, discover, and uncover congruent truths for every aspect of society.

We can apply our gifts to our dreams.

We can be unique and separate as well as being part

of a team, no matter where the rest of our team is located historically (past or future) or geographically. We can still build and grow together, like the Garden City discussed in Chapter 4.

I encourage you to seek out appropriate mentors (even if they are not personally mentoring you, which sometimes can be better) where necessary in each pillar so that you can learn new perspective of congruency for every pillar. I encourage you to go through the process in this book again, maybe while journaling, or with a planned you-time vacation.

I encourage you to take time with this process by meditating on different points with the Holy Spirit and to not let yourself become discouraged if feelings of being unseen or misunderstood creep in again. You are a leader. Stick with your vision, and the rest will follow.

OUR KING AND PRIEST

Christ is our King and Priest, and we are called, "kings and priests to our God."

My dear, you are both a queen and a priest! Not only does the spiritual affect the physical and the physical affect the spiritual, but they are both made of some similar substance: faith!

It does not matter who is agreeing with your spirit right now. You agree with it. It does not matter what societies or nations you see right now. Build with the ones you want to see, or raise up one you want to see with others.

I remember when I first found the book *Urban Acupuncture* by Jaime Lerner. I was so excited to read a book by someone who understood the concept of metaphysics for the good of everyone's enjoyment through daily applications within his field (government and business/ commerce).

From that day forward, I began to intentionally seek out others who had congruent beliefs and who were making an impact. I wanted to learn from them and be like them in my own way.

Do any of them know who I am? Most likely not.

Do I need any of them to know who I am? No. I just need to know the people who I am meant to be connected with, and that is all that matters – making the most of my placement in Christ and enjoying every day of it, as challenges and victories can both be used to expand and multiply what is already within us.

It is our perspective on what actually makes up a society that matters as a Christian. When we know what kind of party it is, we know how it is we are to show up.

Lauren Ahmadian is a businesswoman and former missionary with a vision for societal progress propelled by the love of Christ.

Lauren combines her leadership experience in business and spiritual settings to help people find their best self and claim their place in society. She currently resides in the United States.

LET'S START A MOVEMENT WITH YOUR MESSAGE

In a market where hundreds of thousands of books are published every year and are never heard from again, The Author Incubator is different. Not only do all Difference Press books reach Amazon bestseller status, but all of our authors are actively changing lives and making a difference.

Since launching in 2013, we've served over 500 authors who came to us with an idea for a book and were able to write it and get it self-published in less than 6 months. In addition, more than 100 of those books were picked up by traditional publishers and are now available in bookstores. We do this by selecting the highest quality and highest potential applicants for our future programs.

Our program doesn't only teach you how to write a book – our team of coaches, developmental editors, copy editors, art directors, and marketing experts incubate you from having a book idea to being a published, bestselling author, ensuring that the book you create can actually make a difference in the world. Then we give you the training you need to use your book to make the difference in the world, or to create a business out of serving your readers.

ARE YOU READY TO MAKE A DIFFERENCE?

You've seen other people make a difference with a book. Now it's your turn. If you are ready to stop watching and start taking massive action, go to http://theauthorincubator.com/apply/.

"Yes, I'm ready!"

Dear reader,

Thank you so much for your heart and time as you went through this book. I am sure your spirit and mind are already stirring with the next steps for yourself.

I would love to hear your thoughts and stay in touch. You can contact me through the following venues:

Email – breath@breathbuilds.org
Instagram – breathbuilds
Facebook – breathbuilds
Website (in creation right now)

When contacting me, please mention the book so that I may respond with relevant offers that may occurring at that time.